# Managers, can you hear me now?

## Hard-Hitting Lessons on How to Get Real Results

# DENNY F. STRIGL

### AND FRANK SWIATEK

NEW YORK   CHICAGO   SAN FRANCISCO   LISBON   LONDON
MADRID   MEXICO CITY   MILAN   NEW DELHI   SAN JUAN
SEOUL   SINGAPORE   SYDNEY   TORONTO

1 2 3 4 5 6 7 8 9 1  QFR/QFR  1 5 4 3 2 1

ISBN   978-0-07-175913-7
MHID       0-07-175913-1

McGraw-Hill books are available at special quantity discounts to use as premiums and sales promotions or for use in corporate training programs. To contact a representative, please e-mail us at bulksales@mcgraw-hill.com.

This book is printed on acid-free paper.

This book is dedicated to my three grandsons,
Nathaniel, Harrison, and Grant.

*—Denny*

❖  ❖  ❖

I would like to dedicate this book to my grandchildren—
Connor, Matthew, Jack, Max, Andrew, Sean, Addison, and Evan.
They are all a great source of pride and happiness.

*—Frank*

# Contents

# Foreword

In this innovative and practical guide for frontline managers, Denny explains time-tested techniques and leadership principles that create a sustainable high-performance culture. As Denny's colleague for many years, I have experienced the value and effectiveness of these techniques firsthand. The personal anecdotes and insights throughout the book offer an invaluable teaching tool for every manager trying to balance the difficult task of achieving results the right way—by building a winning team.

Denny's work ethic and high standards inspired generations of managers and helped create a culture of performance that is his lasting legacy to Verizon Communications.

This is an essential read for every manager's, or aspiring manager's, success for one simple reason: it is all authentic and it works.

Ivan G. Seidenberg
Chairman and CEO
Verizon Communications, Inc.

# Acknowledgments

I'm indebted to several people who have contributed to the presentation of the advice we have offered in this book. First, my wife, Amanda, not only inspired me but provided great ideas and sage counsel throughout the process. I couldn't have written this without her help. Second, many of my former colleagues at Verizon were invaluable in their cooperation and support: Ivan Seidenberg, Lowell McAdam, Steve Zipperstein, and, especially, Jim Gerace, who was very helpful in articulating the facts surrounding the birth of the Verizon Wireless credo, which he deserves credit for synthesizing. In addition, Jim was very helpful in reviewing and clarifying several other chapters. I'm likewise grateful for Donald Caplin's help in formulating the discussions of distractions and culture in the book. And a special thanks to copyeditor Steve McCabe, of Wordwright Editorial Services, Inc., for helping us choose the right words and put them in the right order.

And, of course, I'm grateful to my family for the support they have shown for this project. Writing is hard and solitary work, and they have tolerated my absence and forgiven my inattentiveness while I have focused on this project. I appreciate their understanding and hope they will now share in my happiness (and relief) at its completion.

*Denny Strigl, Lake Placid, New York*

❖  ❖  ❖

Coauthoring this book has been the culmination of many organizational experiences and the result of many mentoring relationships. I would like to acknowledge my early mentors who helped me to shape a foundation of management, leadership, and speaking. In particular, Don Deverall and Dennis Eaton of the Waterloo Management Education Centre in Canada; Al and Joan Cannie of Learning Dynamics in Boston; Dr. Ken Lipke; Earl P. Strong of Penn State University; and Dr. Herb True and Bill Gove, speakers extraordinaire.

I would also like to thank Denny Strigl for the opportunity to collaborate on this book. I have worked in his organizations for over 15 years as a performance consultant. I have seen firsthand his ability to develop a dynamic, results-focused company. He is one of the most successful CEOs in corporate America in the last 20 years. And while he believes that it is not "all about him," his willingness to share his powerful beliefs and concepts will have a significant impact on managers and leaders of the future.

Finally, I would like to thank my wife, Betty Anne, for her continuous love and support in all of my professional endeavors.

*Frank Swiatek, Cheektowaga, New York*

# Introduction

Liston Street in Buffalo, New York, was not known as being part of the richest of neighborhoods, but it's where I grew up. I was never much of a student in high school; frankly, I couldn't sit still for more than 10 minutes without getting antsy. As a kid, I was good at sports, but my primary interest was flying airplanes. By the time I was 19 years old, I had a commercial pilot's license.

In 1966, after two years of college, I dropped out and joined the army. After the army, I was on track to become an airline pilot until I found out the pay for starting pilots was only $350 a month. One of my flying buddies suggested I might be able to land a better-paying job in the "business world." I thought it was a pretty dumb idea, but what was there to lose? So on a whim, I walked up and down Main Street in Buffalo one rainy June day in 1968 and filled out job applications at several banks, the water company, the gas company, and the telephone company. New York Telephone offered me a job a few days later at almost twice the pay I would have made as a pilot. (Incidentally, working a regular day job gave me the opportunity to finish college at night, which I did 10 years after I took my first course.)

Forty-one years later, I retired as president and COO of one of the largest telecommunications firms in the world, with operating revenues totaling over $107 billion. Throughout my career, I wore many hats, from telephone installer to salesperson to CEO. I can honestly say that I learned something from every position. At each job I encountered different challenges, with new people and new managers.

Over the years, I sorted my good experiences from the bad ones and came up with the management philosophy that is detailed in this book. You will find much of what is presented here to be contrary to what is taught in business schools and management seminars, or even what you may have learned on the job. What you will read in these pages, however, are field-tested concepts that produce results.

My coauthor is Frank Swiatek. Frank is a performance consultant and speaker who helps managers and organizations improve their results. He has led over 3,400 speaking engagements and seminars throughout the United States and Canada and has worked for more than 25 Fortune 500 companies, including Verizon Wireless. Frank and I are both graduates of Canisius College in Buffalo, New York.

Two months after I retired, Frank sent me an e-mail asking how I was doing. I told him that I was learning how to teach people to fly, which I had always wanted to do, and I was also learning to fly a helicopter, something which I said I would never do. He concluded his e-mail reply by asking if I had ever considered writing a book. I said that I had, and after further discussion, we decided to collaborate.

To tell you the truth, I am not a big fan of consultants. In fact, I have terminated many of them in my career. However, I have always been impressed by how effectively Frank's sessions were aligned with Verizon Wireless and with my thoughts and values as a manager. He has conducted sessions for the company in the areas of improving accountability, commitment, respect, and trust for both managers and employees—all of which are major subjects in this book.

Throughout these pages, you will find that we use numerous real-life examples to reinforce and drive home the concepts we present. I will use Frank's name to identify his stories and examples. Occasionally, you'll find us speaking together as "we" to describe a point or sentiment that we both share.

When Frank and I first talked about writing this book, we decided we wanted to do something different from what authors of business books have done in the past. We have each spent over 40 years working with managers, and we've seen plenty of successful ones in action. All too often, we've also seen managers fail, and we have each drawn conclusions about why they have done so. Our goal is to share as much knowledge with you as we can from our combined experience to help you be an effective and successful manager.

You will find this is not a book detailing some of the "tried-and-true" management techniques you learned in college (I say that with tongue firmly in cheek), or at a seminar, or from reading a management consultant's best-selling book. Neither will we discuss some new management style guaranteed to accelerate you into a senior-level position, nor will we give you the management tactic du jour. Rather, Frank and I will tell you how successful managers act—what they do, what they don't do, and how. We will give you some practical tips and tools, along with plenty of examples reflecting real-world experiences. I will share with you what worked for me, and candidly what did not, as I made my way up the ranks of a major corporation. Frank will share with you his experience as a performance consultant working with organizations throughout the United States and Canada for more than 40 years.

Most of what you will read in this book was never taught in a classroom. Some of what you will read will be contrary to what you have previously learned to do as a manager. However, whether you are a new manager or a veteran with years of experience, it is our hope that what is presented in this book will both debunk management myths that may be impeding your effectiveness and help you become more successful in your career.

## THE MANAGER'S PRIORITY: DELIVER RESULTS

The foundation of our managers' philosophy relies on one main, undeniable point: a manager's number-one priority is to deliver results. A good manager will push all other extraneous issues or distractions aside and figure out what is necessary to reach set goals and objectives.

Good managers will not make excuses. They will not procrastinate. Instead, they will achieve results. Throughout this book you will find us discussing this concept in a number of ways, providing information on how to reach this performance level. We will repeatedly refer to what I call the "Four Fundamentals." These fundamentals should be the focus of all managers. If the things you are doing as a manager don't produce the following results, then you need to stop doing them:

1. Grow revenue.
2. Get new customers.
3. Keep the customers you already have.
4. Eliminate costs.

I try to be very clear when I explain that these four things are what are important, and they are the only things that are important. Simple! Period!

Of course, to utilize the Four Fundamentals does not mean to disregard the law, your employees, or your boss. In fact, the relationship you have with your employees and the culture you build within your company are imperative to the Four Fundamentals. Without a sense of trust and respect between you and your employees, results will not be achieved. Without displaying integrity and maintaining your own sense of this value, whether in public or private, you will not succeed. As a manager, you must be accountable for your behavior and instill this sense of accountability in your employees. As you will see, a major reason that managers struggle is due to a lack of accountable behavior in their organization. This means that those managers fail to set a good example of accountability in their daily operations and, consequently, do not build accountability in their employees.

What we cover in the following chapters will provide you with the foundation to create a results-focused culture within your organization. We will begin by identifying some common reasons managers struggle in their jobs and, ultimately, why they fail. In the chapters that follow, we explore in detail the reasons for failure, let you know how to successfully avoid them, and help you understand how to ultimately meet your obligations by producing results in your company.

## Chapter 1

# Why Managers Struggle

The overall reason managers struggle to be successful in their jobs is their behavior. It is what they *do* or *don't do* that makes them serious performers, marginal performers, or failures. It's all about their behavior; behavior is the key to achievement.

In her 1980 book *Take Charge: Success Tactics for Business and Life*, Joan Koob Cannie, former chairwoman of Learning Dynamics, an industry leader in organizational development, put it this way:

> Research in several areas, psychology, management, and attitude change, shows that the single most important factor in success is behavior, not education or a string of degrees, not intelligence, not experience, or technical expertise—just behavior. And behavior is something we all do, the difference being in only how we do it.[1]

Consider the following three examples:

Have you ever gone to a high school or college reunion and been totally surprised at the level of success that some people have achieved? They may not necessarily have been on the honor roll or had the highest grade point averages. They weren't the class officers or the most popular students. They certainly were not voted most likely to succeed, but they did so in their careers, and sometimes in very big ways.

Many managers I have encountered are seminar junkies. They attend all the latest and greatest management and leadership programs. However, when you look at their results, you would never know they ever attended even one program. They have a huge gap between what they know and what they actually do.

I have also met many newly appointed managers, some of whom made a great first impression. They spoke the language of success. They had a wonderful personal bearing and seemed to be a "package" that could not possibly fail. However, over the years, as I followed their careers, they never became exceptional performers despite all the advantages they apparently possessed at the outset.

These examples point out the truth in Joan Koob Cannie's assertion: it is *behavior*—based on skill, drive, persistence, and ambition—that creates management success. But it is not just behavior alone. It is behavior that is repeated until it becomes habit. Exceptional managers do the same things, day in and day out, creating positive results.

## SPECIFIC REASONS MANAGERS STRUGGLE

It is easy enough to say behavior is the overall reason managers struggle and leave it at that. However, to understand the deeper reasons managers face so many issues, we must explore their specific behaviors—the things they do and don't do.

## *Reason Number 1: Managers Fail to Build Trust and Integrity*

The first reason managers struggle is that they fail to build trust initially or they erode trust with their employees during daily interactions and operations. Trust is the glue that binds managers and employees. If the employees don't believe in the messengers, they certainly won't believe in the messages!

A key leadership priority is to create an environment where trust can flourish. It is incumbent upon managers to hold themselves accountable for the level of trust that exists in their department or organization. A key obligation of managers is to cultivate the faith and respect of those who report to them.

Here are some examples of manager behaviors that build trust:

▶ Saying what you mean and meaning what you say
▶ Seeking input and feedback from your team
▶ Treating people with dignity
▶ Being dependable in meeting commitments
▶ Creating clear focus and objectives for people
▶ Creating a climate of open, honest, and
   direct communications

Without trust, there can be little cooperation among coworkers and between departments. This situation will result in little risk taking that could otherwise prove fruitful, less employee empowerment, a lack of commitment among employees and to the organization, diminished confidence in employees, and a loss of genuine communication throughout the company. Results will be seriously hampered in such a trust-averse environment.

Here are some examples of manager behaviors that build distrust:

▶ Lack of openness with employees
▶ Micromanaging
▶ Lack of respect in communications
▶ Lack of integrity and honesty
▶ Self-serving, hidden agendas
▶ Words and actions that are not consistent

Failure to build trust and integrity will result in a very low level of commitment from employees; in turn, they will often do just enough to stay on the job.

## Reason Number 2: They Have the Wrong Focus

Managers who struggle spend too much time focused on things that don't really matter. For example, they may waste time preparing useless reports nobody reads. It is also possible for managers to get hung up on bureaucratic and nonsensical issues that often get institutionalized in companies. Some may even go to extraneous meetings that are of little or no value to them in an effort to avoid "real" work that actually produces results. Other managers stick themselves behind their desks, writing reports or pushing papers because that is what they are most comfortable doing.

Add to these examples the number of distractions managers face every day due to constant interruptions caused by ready access to electronic devices. Managers can easily get absorbed with e-mail, text messages, phone calls, and phone messages—most of which keep them from focusing on what is really important.

I always tell managers to stop doing things that don't matter! You will find people sometimes complain that they "have to" attend a meeting, file a report, or even go to a training

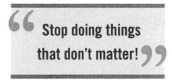

Stop doing things that don't matter!

program. My response is always the same: if it doesn't fit into one of the Four Fundamentals: growing revenue, getting new customers, keeping the customers they already have, or eliminating costs (discussed in the Introduction and detailed in Chapter 3), they should rethink what they're doing.

You will find that when enough of your employees get this message, the news about what you consider important will spread quickly. Productivity will improve, and so will results. But remember one note of caution: unless you, the manager, continually reinforce the Four Fundamentals and what's important, unnecessary activities will always creep back in.

### *Reason Number 3: They Don't Model or Build Accountability*

It is critical for the manager to be *the* model of accountability in daily operations. Managers need to realize their behavior is in a "fishbowl" and thereby highly visible for their employees to see and imitate. Employees watch their manager in all situations, but especially when the manager is under stress. What the manager says and does in stressful situations sends a signal to all employees to imitate that behavior, even when they are not under stress. If a manager blames or bashes others, becomes sarcastic, or makes unethical choices under stress, that manager is setting a tone of unaccountability in his or her department—a tone that will have a negative impact on results.

Accountable behavior is at the heart of achieving results. Such behavior includes:

▶ Taking action
▶ Making decisions
▶ Being proactive
▶ Owning issues and problems
▶ Demonstrating commitment
▶ Rising above circumstances
▶ Taking extra steps to get results

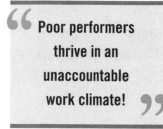

> **Poor performers thrive in an unaccountable work climate!**

Here is something I have discovered: *poor performers thrive in an unaccountable work climate!* Why? Because they never take responsibility for missing a deadline, not achieving a positive result, making a poor decision, or taking an action that backfires. There is always something or someone for them to blame, and they continually have an excuse. Unaccountable behavior is at the root of this poor performance and includes behaviors such as:

▶ Blaming others
▶ Rationalizing poor results
▶ Making excuses
▶ Ducking issues
▶ Whining
▶ Letting things slide

It is important for the manager to build accountability in others as he or she attempts to improve performance. Specifically, managers must reinforce the concept of accountability through feedback, coaching, and performance tools. Using accountability as a consistent message in your feedback comments to employees, and in your coaching sessions with them, will go a long way toward letting all employees know accountable behavior is expected in your organization.

A variety of performance tools signal the importance of accountability in employee behavior. Clear performance measurements and milestones and well-explained objectives help ensure accountability for an employee's actions, behaviors, and results. With goals established, performance becomes as clear as your bowling score or your golf score—no one has to tell you how well you are doing; it's there for you to see. You have a set of visible metrics that you are accountable for, providing you with ongoing feedback on your performance.

You can also use a variety of reporting techniques to help you achieve an accountable work climate. End-of-week "5:15 Reports," for example, will help track both your and your employees' progress on the way to achieving results. Performance agreements such as these will clearly set expectations for the results that you and your employees are accountable for. Market and operational reviews will also formalize the reporting on accountable objectives, while tough questions and uncomfortable conversations during these reviews help ensure accountability. Finally, when accountable objectives are off track, performance improvement plans will help reestablish them through an action plan.

We will define and provide additional information on these tools, with specific examples, in Chapter 6.

## Reason Number 4: They Fail to Consistently Reinforce What's Important

The fourth reason managers struggle is they fail to reinforce what's important. It sounds obvious, but I have found that it's not always easy to do. Managers often stress a particular message, a goal, a tactic, or a program, for a couple of weeks. Once they think their people "get it," they believe they don't need to talk about it anymore.

Unfortunately, they are wrong.

When managers assume their people get it is when "it" starts to be forgotten. Employees watch carefully to see what their manager thinks is important in an effort to please their boss. When managers stop reinforcing something, it usually signals to their employees that either it's not important anymore or it's not as important as it once was.

Another reason managers stop reinforcing something that's important is because they get tired of saying the same thing, and delivering the same message, over and over again. I've always cautioned managers that they are the ones who often will be the first to get bored with their message. However, don't let your own boredom cause you to change your message.

When managers change their message too often, people become confused about what's important. They wonder whether your last message was the one that was most important, or whether this one is, or whether the next one will be—what I call the "message du jour syndrome." The people who work for you perform best when what you say is consistent and frequent.

## Reason Number 5: They Overrely on Consensus

Many times, managers struggle because they try to become consensus builders. They go to a lot of effort to get agreement from others before they make decisions or take action. These are the managers who like to touch every base and obtain agreement from everyone before moving ahead. In order to reach consensus, they usually alter their plans or modify their proposal in some way. To get the buy-in from everyone they work with, they will likely end up with a watered-down version of the original decision or action they intended.

These are the same managers who overrely on consensus, taking them much more time than it should to reach a conclusion on how to proceed. Consensus managers seldom survive long in their jobs, especially if they work for companies operating in highly competitive markets. In such markets, decisions must be made quickly to respond to rapidly changing market conditions. Generally, I have found consensus managers hesitate to take action because they lack confidence in their own decision-making abilities. They are afraid of making a mistake. If many others are brought into the process, however, and the consensus-building manager ends up making a mistake, he or she is comforted by the thought that the blame will be shared.

Here's an example to help clarify this concept.

If I'm a consensus manager, I want all the people with whom I work to agree to a course of action I propose, and if they don't agree at first, I will simply modify my position until they do. Ironically, what we all finally agree to may be so compromised that it might not accomplish what I initially set out to do.

Let's say I'm a district retail manager. I'm responsible for 10 of my company's stores located in the western portion of my state. Ten store managers report to me. We are experiencing a very slow period, and I am far off my sales targets for the quarter. I badly need to boost my results before the quarter's end, which is quickly approaching. So I propose a plan to get more shoppers into our stores by mailing a $10 gift certificate to those we consider our best customers, based on their previous purchases. The gift certificate would be applied to all purchases over $100 completed before the end of the quarter.

When I ask my store managers to agree to the plan, three of them say $10 is not enough, three say they want the $10 gift certificates to apply only to specific products, and the four remaining managers don't want to do anything because they are already meeting their sales targets for the quarter.

In order to reach consensus, I compromise by proposing a $15 gift certificate that customers can apply to a half dozen of our products. Six of my managers are satisfied. I also tell the four managers who are meeting their sales targets that they are not required to participate. The good news? I have reached consensus! The bad news? I've lost time getting my plan implemented. I've also caused customer confusion, since customers can use their gift certificates only in six specific stores. In the end, I have probably missed my sales targets for the quarter.

> **"It is more important to take action, even if it is imperfect, than do nothing."**

I have always believed it is more important to take action, even if it is imperfect, than do nothing. Inaction or delayed action is a much bigger mistake than moving ahead, even though the action taken may need to be modified in the future. It's okay, in my book, for well-intentioned managers to make a mistake as long as they recognize their mistake quickly and take appropriate corrective steps.

I'd like to be clear that it is, of course, important to research your decisions and call upon the best resources possible to help you understand and reach the most appropriate courses of action. However, such informed decision making is much different to me than the counterproductive consensus-building process described above.

I have worked for several consensus-building managers over my career. They were nice people. They meant well. Unfortunately, managing results was not the job they were cut out to do. Eventually, they missed their objectives, and they lost the respect of the very employees with whom they worked to reach consensus on nearly every decision.

### Reason Number 6: They Focus on Being Popular

The first priority of a manager is to deliver results. It is not about building friendships. Early on, managers learn that it's important to focus on the people who work for them. I agree: it is always important to focus on one's employees, but that focus is not on being their friend, nor is it necessarily on making them happy— which is a mistake a lot of managers make.

The first priority of a manager is to deliver results. It is not about building friendships.

Think of it this way: happy employees don't necessarily bring you stellar results, although I would argue that stellar results often bring happy, or at least satisfied, employees.

When results are achieved, pride builds. When pride builds, so does confidence. With confidence comes the desire to do even better. Trust and loyalty then grow. Good managers understand this process and therefore "drive" results, giving little care to building personal friendships with employees. Instead, these managers want trust and loyalty, which is exactly what sustained performance gets them.

Here's a note to new managers: I've found that your employees, most likely, will not trust you, or even like you, at first. You may find they will want to do things the old, comfortable way even if it doesn't lead to positive results or if they aren't totally realizing their potential. University of Southern California business professor and author Warren G. Bennis calls this the "unconscious conspiracy"—the tendency for people not only to want to keep things the same but also to unconsciously undermine efforts to change. Of course, some employees will also consciously attempt to do so.

Good managers don't worry about shaking up the status quo or unintentionally "hurting" people's feelings, because they know all the employees will "feel good" later when results are achieved, not missed. Those managers who prefer to avoid confrontation and change within an organization end up harboring employees who stay comfy, don't get results, and wallow in their lack of performance, but love their boss over the short term for being so "reasonable and understanding." Over the longer term, however, morale suffers, commiseration runs rampant, targets continue to be missed, people resign—or, worse yet, they quit trying but stay with the company—and, of course, eventually a new manager shows up.

The bottom line is this: leadership should never be a popularity contest. Managers who try to be popular often lose their focus and waste energy. Remember, *results are what matter*!

## Reason Number 7: They Get Caught Up in Their Self-Importance

Another reason managers struggle is due to what I like to call the "all-about-me" syndrome. I often find that managers who fail do so because they get caught up in the "aura" of their position and become hung up on their own self-importance. They seek recognition and often glamour for themselves. These are the people who can't wait to read their own name in print or see their picture in the newspaper. They love to give speeches to groups and in places that don't really matter. These managers look forward to playing golf with suppliers and vendors and enjoying "business" lunches and dinners. I think you get the picture. In my opinion, none of this kind of behavior is important or productive, and it most likely distracts from the manager's real job: achieving results. Managers who suffer from the all-about-me syndrome seldom see that what is causing their own demise is their diminishing attention to what is important and their growing infatuation with what isn't.

When I started my career with New York Telephone in Buffalo, New York, I observed a sales manager who clearly suffered from the all-about-me syndrome. Each year the company would hire a small number of Ivy League college graduates and place them into an accelerated "fast-track" management development program. These individuals were the best and the brightest of their graduating class. During the hiring process, they were informed that if they came to work for New York Telephone, they would be trained to become senior-level managers in the company. They would be placed in various individual assignments that lasted from six months to a year. After several of these assignments over a period of years, they were guaranteed promotions to mid-level management positions followed by additional promotions until they reached the top-management ranks.

The sales manager I observed was a participant in this fast-track program. We all knew he was in the program—primarily because he told us about it at every opportunity! He would repeatedly remind us of his college credentials and his special status as a member of this fast-track development program. He also would let us know that he only expected to be in our department for a short time. He thoroughly enjoyed talking about himself.

Of course, it wasn't long before he was widely disliked.

The one thing we did like about him was that he wasn't in the office much. He spent much of his time introducing himself and presenting his résumé to mid-level and senior-level managers all around New York State.

Six months came and went, as did his first full year with the company. While other participants in the fast-track program had moved on to a second and third job, he was still a sales manager. In addition to having a problem of being disliked by his peers and sales representatives, his sales results were the poorest in the area. Before his second anniversary with the company, he wisely decided to seek employment elsewhere.

Here was an employee who, by all appearances, could have quickly moved up the ranks of the company, but because of his behavior— being so focused on himself—he missed the fact that he actually had to achieve results in order to be considered for his next promotion.

> **A truly good manager knows "it's *not* about me."**

The best managers I've worked with are too busy driving results to seek recognition for themselves. When positive recognition does come, they make sure it's focused on their company, their organization, and their team— in other words, on the people they work with. A truly good manager knows "it's *not* about me."

### *Reason Number 8: They Put Their Heads in the Sand*

Many managers struggle because they only want to hear good news. It would be nice if there were always only positive news to report, but of course, this isn't the case. These "good-news-only" managers create a work environment that encourages good news and punishes bad news. This is the type of environment in which, when employees bring problems or issues to their boss, he or she either refuses to take the time to listen or ignores the problem and allows it to persist. I remember one boss of mine who actually said, "The good things we do are mine. The problems are yours. I don't want to hear any of your problems!"

Employees who work for good-news-only managers quickly learn to report positive information, while hiding any problems. As a result, productivity suffers, employee morale decreases, and targeted results are missed. The environment created by good-news-only managers can lead to disastrous consequences, and when you are afraid to tell your boss the truth, trouble can result for you, your organization, and your company. There are even instances in which employees have attempted to avoid telling their managers about negative financial results by reporting fictitious financial results to the public.

The best managers I've worked with, however, not only want to hear about problems, but encourage their employees to tell them when they encounter problems or issues they feel are not right. Good managers want open, honest, direct, and specific communication regardless of the information being presented.

### Reason Number 9: They Fix Problems, Not Causes

The ninth reason managers struggle is because they fix a problem without addressing the reason the problem occurred. Unless managers fix the causes of the problems they experience, it is very likely the problems will reoccur. Managers may then find themselves constantly putting out fires. Valuable time will be spent fixing the same problem over and over again, which can become a huge source of frustration.

In most cases, this situation occurs due to three issues:

1. The manager doesn't have the time to immediately address the cause of the problem. A manager's failure to take the time to fix the cause of a problem ignores the fact that the problem will

simply keep coming back. It is much more effective and efficient to address the problem and get it resolved immediately, even if it means the manager's attention must be taken away from other important tasks!

2. The manager doesn't have the resources to address the cause of the problem. I recognize that, in the real world, resource constraints are a significant issue that managers grapple with continually, but to avoid a reoccurring problem, resources must be found to address its cause. As discussed previously, it is much more resource-efficient to fix the problem's cause as soon as possible. Maybe it can't be done immediately, and maybe it can't be done all the time, but it must be done diligently to conserve time and resources in the future.

3. The manager believes that the problem is beyond his or her control. I have often heard managers say the cause of a given problem is not within their control. In other words, it's someone else's issue to fix. For example, the cause may be in another function or organization in the company. This way of thinking is very short-sighted. A manager can point a finger at someone or something else and place blame, but it still doesn't solve the problem once and for all. The manager needs to "force" the right things to happen. Managers who have a desire to fix problems and their causes can almost always find the means to do so.

As we wrote this chapter, I thought back on my own experiences with managers who struggled in their jobs and who were ultimately removed from their management roles and either reassigned to different positions within the company or asked to leave the company entirely. Every one of these managers I can think of who was reassigned or terminated struggled because of one of the nine reasons described in this chapter. Now that we have covered the basics about why managers have difficulty in their jobs, we will turn our attention to the details of the impediments behind struggling managers and focus on how managers can break free of them and ultimately become successful.

## Chapter Summary Points

1. Behavior is the key to achievement. It is what managers do or don't do that makes them successful, mediocre, or a failure.
2. Managers must change their behavior in order to stop struggling and become successful.
3. Exceptional managers are results-focused, first and foremost. They are consistent. They rely on practicing the same successful behaviors, day in and day out.

## Chapter Action Guide

Now that we have reviewed the nine reasons managers struggle, I'd like to offer an opportunity for a self-evaluation. If you're a new manager, or a veteran manager who would like to refresh your skills, take a few moments to respond to the questions that follow. Your answers will help you identify the specific chapters of the book where your interests and priorities may lie and give you an idea of the opportunities that you have to be a better manager.

### *Where Do I Stand?*

Behavior: What You Do or Don't Do
Can you identify specific management behaviors—new things that you are doing or not doing—that you put into practice over the last year?

## *Nine Reasons Managers Fail: How Do You Stack Up?*

### Reason Number 1: They Fail to Build Trust and Integrity

Do you say and do things that erode trust within your work climate?

### Reason Number 2: They Have the Wrong Focus

Do you feel you are wasting time, effort, and money by focusing on things that just don't matter in getting results?

### Reason Number 3: They Don't Model or Build Accountability

Do you have a tendency to blame others, point fingers, or look for excuses?

### Reason Number 4: They Fail to Consistently Reinforce What's Important

Do you have a core performance message—like the Four Fundamentals—that you constantly talk about with your employees?

### Reason Number 5: They Overrely on Consensus

Do you find that your decisions are delayed or end up watered down because of your overemphasis on consensus?

### Reason Number 6: They Focus on Being Popular

Do you feel a strong desire to be liked, to be popular, and to befriend people, and is this having a negative effect on your management results?

### Reason Number 7: They Get Caught Up in Their Self-Importance

Do you have a high need to gain admiration, be in the spotlight, and get public accolades?

### Reason Number 8: They Put Their Heads in the Sand

Do you react poorly to bad news, hide it, or dismiss it?

### Reason Number 9: They Fix Problems, Not Causes

Do you tend to fix problems with Band-Aid solutions rather than seek and eradicate the root cause of the problem, even if it may lie in another area?

## Chapter 2

# The Power of Trust: Integrity, Openness, and Respect

Trust is a vital management ingredient, the foundation of success not only for the manager, but for the enterprise as a whole. I feel so strongly about this concept, I wanted "trust" to be the book's first main principle we delve into. All other pieces of a manager's job are built upon trust.

I offer this chapter to focus on how the three major qualities of trust are facilitators of success: integrity, openness, and respect. Without these qualities, companies and managers can still survive—although it's getting a lot tougher—but they certainly will not achieve the same results they can with them.

When I use the word "trust," I'm describing a workplace in which employees can rely on their managers to create, build, and maintain a sense of confidence and belief in their daily operations and over-all effectiveness. Effective managers trust the employees they work

> " **Building trust always begins with the manager.** "

with implicitly, and they will continue to do so unless these employees prove themselves undeserving of it. Likewise, effective managers have the trust of their employees, but this is not a "chicken-or-the-egg" question—building trust always begins with the manager. The manager is the initiator of trust in the function, department, or organization. Employees want to be led by managers they can trust.

The best-performing managers I've met had the trust not only of their employees but also of their bosses and their internal and external peers. Bosses could absolutely depend on these managers' words and actions. Internally, they had the trust of other departments they interacted with on a daily basis. Externally, they earned the trust of their customers, suppliers, and vendors.

## THE THREE MAJOR QUALITIES OF TRUST

Trust is a powerful ally. As managers, we gain the trust of our employees through the three major qualities mentioned previously: when we operate with integrity, when we are open with our employees, and when we treat them with respect.

### *The First Quality: Integrity*

Though "integrity" is often used as a synonym for "honesty," and has unfortunately been trivialized by a parade of CEOs sent to jail for lacking it, when we use the word "integrity" in this chapter, we mean more than just honesty. We mean an adherence to moral and ethical principles. My way of thinking about this is simple: a manager with integrity is someone who will do the right thing even when no one is watching.

As managers we often find ourselves in situations in which there are opportunities to cut corners, and in any job there are times when we can take unethical or inappropriate actions that no one else may know about. Perhaps it's telling a "little white lie" to make a sale, falsifying a report to make results look better, or padding an expense account. Managers with integrity will always do the right thing, regardless of whether or not they are being watched or think they are being watched. Integrity must be a core value of every manager.

Honesty is a critical but not an exclusive component of integrity. Frankly, I have known managers without integrity who were nonetheless truthful—as in, "Yes, I took the money from the vault." Managers who have integrity earn the respect and trust of the people they work with. Their coworkers see their moral and ethical behavior, as well as witness their honesty, and develop trust toward them.

I told managers who worked with me I expected them to be honest at all times, in everything they did, without exception, *always*! I also told them I would never lie to them, never bluff them, and never "spin" things to make problems or issues appear better or different than they really were.

In the event I suspected someone working for me was fibbing, I always took him or her to task. If, for example, John told me he didn't finish an assignment on time because Mary didn't get him the information he needed to complete it, I would tell John that getting this information was his responsibility. I would then go on to say that, to give him the benefit of the doubt, we should call Mary right now and ask her why she didn't get him what he needed to complete the task. The response I usually got from people like John was, "No, no, don't do that. I'll take care of it right away." In other words, John's unfinished assignment really wasn't Mary's fault at all.

Let's think about this for a minute. When everyone in a work group understands that honesty at all times is the way everyone within the group will operate, it eliminates a lot of uncertainty. No one has to wonder what people really meant when they said something, nor does anyone have to attempt to "read between the lines" with any communication or have to question whether coworkers will really do what they said they would do. When honesty is the standard, guesswork and speculation are no longer necessary. Much interoffice gossip about who said what can be eliminated. Hidden agendas, or disguised plans with ulterior motives, are eliminated. In the case of John, a typical excuse for procrastination is easily exposed. The wasted time saved and redeployed on important work that matters can be enormous!

> " If you've built the foundation of your organization upon integrity, employees will feel they must replicate it to succeed. "

There is no more powerful impact a leader can make on an organization than that made through integrity. Members of the organization will respect their managers and will want to replicate their values. If you've built the foundation of your organization upon integrity, employees will feel they must replicate it to succeed.

Conversely, a fast way to lose the trust of employees is for managers to demonstrate they lack integrity. Trust can take a long time to build, but it can be lost in a single event when integrity has been violated, and it is extremely difficult, sometimes impossible, to regain.

A manager's integrity is tested every day in some way or another. Often it's a simple or seemingly inconsequential challenge. No matter what the test, employees are watching to see how their manager reacts and to determine whether he or she passes.

Each year when I was the president of Bell Atlantic Mobile, a predecessor company of Verizon Wireless, about 200 of the company's top-performing sales representatives were selected to attend an awards and recognition trip based on their results during the prior year. The trip was most often an all-expenses-paid four-day event at an exotic Caribbean location or an exclusive ski resort. On the final evening, a formal awards banquet was held. All the winners were individually recognized in a special ceremony, and the company's top sales representative was announced and honored at the event. As the company president, I gave a speech extolling the virtues of the winner and presented him or her with a Waterford crystal "Eagle Award."

At one such awards banquet, the young man who received the Eagle Award was ecstatic, and the audience gave him a standing ovation for the recognition and appreciation he deserved.

Two weeks later, the head of our human resources department informed me that our Eagle Award recipient had forged several customers' signatures on sales contracts, in clear violation of our company policy.

Over the next 24 hours, I spoke to several members of our management team to help inform the decision I had to make. Most people I talked to recommended disciplinary action that should be nothing more than a mild rebuke, a slap on the wrist. One person even told me to drop the whole matter and do nothing because the individual was our best salesman. As I thought about what I had to do, I knew whatever action I took could set a precedent for how our employees would behave in the future.

My decision was to terminate our Eagle Award–winning "best" sales representative.

In the final analysis, it made no difference to me what his results were or how "valuable" he might be to us in the future. To do anything other than fire him would have sent the wrong message to employees throughout the company. To allow him to remain with Bell Atlantic Mobile would signal that the company's president condoned cheating.

When I was a new mid-level manager working in the training department at AT&T, several people reported directly to me. Our job was to conduct research and write training courses. As a manager, I had to review and approve the expense reports of employees who worked for me—including those traveling as part of our training-course development efforts.

During my first month on the job, I noticed that the expenses of one of my employees were running significantly higher than those of others in my group. Since his expenses seemed out of line with my other employees, I reviewed each of his expense reports from the preceding three months. At first, everything seemed in order, but a closer look revealed duplicate receipts for the same expense, such as an original car rental receipt submitted on one expense report and a copy of that same receipt on a subsequent report. I then looked at his expense reports for the preceding six months and found duplicate car rental, hotel, and meal receipts throughout them. He had overreported expenses in the amount of several thousand dollars.

Dealing with a situation like this was completely foreign to me, so I asked my boss for advice. His reaction stunned me: he said I should forget about it. He told me a lot of people inflate their expense reports to cover for the time they are required to spend away from home. When I told him he was wrong and this was not something I could simply forget about, he became angry with me. When I left his office, I reported my findings to the AT&T security department and requested it investigate the situation.

The next day, a security officer called me and asked me to meet with him in his office, where he and another officer interviewed me for two hours. At the end of the interview, they told me to tell absolutely no one about the investigation. I knew I had done the right thing, but I was certain my boss would fire me when he found out I had reported the situation. It also crossed my mind that our security department might investigate not only my employee's expense reports but the expense reports of several other employees in our department. If the problem was widespread, as my boss had implied, many people would be affected. I felt terrible about the whole situation.

The security department's investigation lasted more than two months—the longest two months of my career. At the close of the investigation, the security officer called me and asked me to meet him in a conference room in the security office. When I arrived, I was shown thousands of pieces of paper, all evidence detailing the crime committed by my employee. He had stolen more than $10,000. The security officer told me the employee had been escorted to the same conference room an hour earlier, been confronted with the evidence, and admitted his guilt. Needless to say, he was terminated and threatened with criminal prosecution if he failed to return every dollar he had stolen.

The next day, my boss thanked me for my persistence in the matter, and the head of my department sent me a letter of commendation and called me personally to thank me for my integrity.

Managers will find there are times when it is difficult to do the right thing. There may be pressure to look the other way or even bosses who push their managers to do the wrong thing. But the lesson regarding integrity is simple: always do the right thing, whether or not someone is watching.

## *The Second Quality: Openness*

Creating an "open" work environment is a prerequisite to building trust. But what, exactly, *is* an open work environment, and how can managers create it?

An open work environment is one in which employees can speak their minds without fear of reprisal. They not only are free to express their "real" thoughts, but are encouraged to do so. They know their thoughts will be heard. Also, in an open environment, managers accept "bad" news. In fact, when things go wrong, managers will definitely want to hear about it.

Many valuable tools are available to help managers create and nurture an open work environment. Here are the three best:

1. **Get out of the office.** The best and easiest tools to use in creating an open work environment are the manager's own two legs. I learned early in my career that the worst place to be as a manager was behind my desk. When managers get out of their offices and visit employees at all levels in their organizations, they can instantly demonstrate they are open to new ideas, want to learn about issues, are eager to find solutions to problems, and are engaged and interested in the people within their organizations. Visits also send a message to the people on the front lines that they are important and that the boss cares enough to show up and take an interest in their contributions.

2. **Use an open door policy.** The idea behind this tool is simple: the manager tells employees the door to his or her office is always open, and employees are encouraged to come speak with the manager whenever they have something to say. A word of caution: if you say you have an open door, you really *do* have to

keep the door to your office open. At first, your employees won't believe you are serious. They will test you. If they find your office door closed, or if they come into your office and you don't take the time to truly listen to them, word will spread quickly that you weren't serious and your open door policy is a sham. It is also critical to establish in the beginning that while employees are free to express their thoughts and concerns in this open environment, it does not mean that everything they say will be acted upon.

When establishing an open door policy, it is important that all employees know they are welcome, not just those who report directly to the manager. In other words, open door policies work best when all the people in your organization, regardless of title or level, understand they are free to come speak with you. Also, to say, "We have a policy of openness," but then allow managers to sit in their offices all day with their doors shut doesn't jibe. Employees often hear what you say, but in the end it's what you *do* that matters. With an open door policy, as with almost any management tool, *it's the actions behind the words that are critical.*

> 66 **With an open door policy, as with almost any management tool,** *it's the actions behind the words that are critical.* 99

3. **Encourage the obligation of constructive dissent.** This concept is a bit more complex and often misunderstood unless it's continually reinforced. The manager informs employees that as members of the manager's organization, every employee not only has the right to disagree or voice differing opinions, but is *obligated* to do so. In other words, if anyone in the organization believes something is wrong, that person is required to say so.

Notice the use of the adjective "constructive" modifying "dissent"; when an individual exercises the obligation to dissent, it must always be done constructively—that is, in a helpful rather than a hurtful manner. When explaining the obligation of constructive dissent, it is important, too, to explain that when all constructive dissent is heard and considered and a decision is made on how to proceed, employees have a further obligation to accept the decision, rally behind it, and support whatever outcome is sought. Dissent ends when all constructive advice has been weighed and a decision made. Because an employee may have dissented does not entitle that person to *not* support a manager's decision. It takes a lot of discipline to stop arguing "your" side after a decision has gone against you, but that is part of the "obligation" of constructive dissent.

When there is openness in an organization, people can share their real thoughts, and they can say things without fear of reprisal. Trust grows in an open work environment, and so does creativity.

## The Third Quality: Respect

Why do some managers who are otherwise full of potential suddenly start to "derail" from their careers? These are often managers who plan for career advancement, and are anticipated to be able to do so, but are knocked off the tracks and demoted, plateaued, or even terminated. According to research published by Jean Brittain Leslie and Ellen Van Velsor in their 1996 book *A Look at Derailment Today: Europe and North America*, this occurs in as many as 30 to 50 percent of high-potential managers.[1] The research points to one of the key reasons derailment occurs: poor treatment of others.

Specifically, these are managers who are treating others with disrespect by demeaning, belittling, devaluing, or patronizing them. These managers may even be abrasive, dictatorial, mean-spirited, or hostile. In other words, despite everything else going for them, they still lack civility in the workplace.

This issue is escalating, according to Christine Pearson and Christine Porath, coauthors of the book *The Cost of Bad Behavior: How Incivility Is Damaging Your Business and What to Do about It.* Pearson and Porath maintain that 50 percent of employees reported experiencing incivility at work at least once a week.[2] Think about how much time the consequences of this behavior are wasting. In such instances, the managers are creating incivility or are permitting it to occur. In either case, the managers are demonstrating a lack of accountability by not ensuring that respect is part of the culture of their function, organization, or company.

We now come to the proverbial fork in the road in our discussion of respect with two key questions:

1. Do you sacrifice results when you take the road to respect?
2. Must you be disrespectful toward others to get results from them?

My answer to both these questions is a resounding no!

As you are aware by now, I have certain expectations of managers. I demand that managers:

▶ Be accountable
▶ Have a strong focus on results
▶ Take action
▶ Make decisions

▶ Level with me

▶ Face reality and not sweep bad news under the rug

> **Any work climate that focuses on results must also possess respect. You don't have to be tough-talking to be tough-minded.**

Some people mistakenly view this as a cold-hearted management approach, one in which the focus on the task is so strong that civility is largely absent from the work climate. *This is simply not true.* Any work climate that focuses on results must also possess respect. Respect for people is one of my core values. You don't have to be tough-talking to be tough-minded.

Let's look at three practical strategies for demonstrating respect in the workplace.

## Demonstrating Respect by Empowering Employees

Good managers assign employees responsibilities, projects, and initiatives while giving them the authority to fulfill these duties in unfettered ways. Good managers also provide employees with clear direction on the results or outcomes expected. They discuss ideas, encourage and answer questions as they arise, and provide any clarification that may be necessary—and then they get out of the way. In doing so, managers show respect for their employees and their ability to do their jobs.

Some managers I've known who struggled in their positions had a tendency to overmanage or even micromanage. They gave people assignments but actually did most of the work themselves. Others had a tendency to hover over people. These managers truly did not empower their employees. As a result, employees felt disrespected and wondered why their manager didn't trust them to get the job done. When these employees did get something accomplished, they wondered when their boss would begin second-guessing them or redoing their work. This type of situation erodes trust and robs employees of positive energy by always casting doubts in their minds about the work they are performing. Managers who take on the work themselves end up undermining their employees.

I've always told my managers to support their teams in every way possible, short of actually doing their employees' jobs. Sometimes, it's very difficult for managers not to take the work onto themselves, particularly when it needs to be done quickly. William Oncken, Jr., in his classic book *Managing Management Time: Who's Got the Monkey?* warns managers of this practice. He uses a "monkey concept" to drive home the point, defining a "monkey" as the next step in a task that requires time and effort.[3]

For example, if an employee comes to a manager with an issue, the employee might say, "We have a problem!" If the employee then describes the situation and the manager says, "I'll look into it and get back to you," the manager has just picked up a monkey and put it on his back because the next step in finding a solution is now his responsibility.

Oncken affirms that managers are compulsive "monkey picker-uppers" and too often do the work that employees should be empowered to do. The manager ultimately feels overwhelmed and stressed out, while the employee is discontented by not being empowered to solve the problem.

Let's stretch the example a little bit to show how convoluted this practice of picking up monkeys can become. The employee, at some point, may want the monkey back, to complete the task. He or she goes to the manager and says, "Have you thought about the problem we discussed?" The manager states, "I've been really busy, but I'll get back to you by Thursday." The employee has just reversed roles with the manager! The manager is now reporting to the employee and giving the employee a timeline on when the problem will be solved.

My advice is simple: keep the monkeys on the backs of the employees, where they belong. Do this by making sure employees—and not you—take the next steps toward solving their problems by deciding what to do and taking actions in their areas of responsibility. Yes, you can provide guidance by suggesting options or alternatives, but have your employees make the final choices and do the work.

You want your employees to have the freedom to make some of their own decisions and take action on their own. Allowing them to do so demonstrates your respect for them and their capabilities. When managers empower their teams to get their jobs done, give them guidance where necessary, and support them in every way possible short of doing the work themselves, then mutual respect and trust tends to grow.

## Showing Respect When Dealing with Performance Issues

When you have an environment focused on results, it's critical to address performance issues quickly. When an employee is missing targets, the manager must act to correct the course and get the employee back on track. Though avoidance by managers to address these issues is common, it is not the best policy. Managers often avoid such performance discussions because of factors we have talked about: they befriend employees, are concerned about making an employee upset, or prefer good-news conversations rather than bad-news ones.

The challenge for the manager, therefore, is to develop the skills and motivation necessary to facilitate effective performance discussions leading to better, more productive behavior by the employee.

The key skill in resolving these matters is the actual initiation of the performance discussion. Most managers know what they want to talk about in the meeting, but they rarely spend time on how they are going to open the conversation, nor do they think about the specific words they are going to use. As a result, they often improvise the opening, and poor results tend to follow.

Why? Because the opening words often sound disrespectful. The conversation results in the creation of two separate agendas—the manager's and the employee's. The manager's agenda is to refocus the employee on productive behavior and finish the conversation quickly. The employee's is to recover his or her sense of self-esteem and self-worth.

Employees often become defensive and start to rationalize and make excuses for their lack of performance. They will also try to recover their self-esteem by focusing on all the good things they have accomplished, while not being terribly interested in discussing their performance weaknesses. Nor will they be interested in ending the conversation as quickly as the manager. This is exactly how performance discussions go awry, with very little good coming out of them.

To keep performance discussions focused and productive, I recommend taking a few minutes to plan your opening remarks carefully, using these principles:

▶ **Know your state of mind going into the performance discussion.** Your state of mind has to be right for the performance discussion to be productive. If you are extremely upset or angry and you want to rip into somebody, your attitude is disrespectful and is likely not to produce the long-term results you want from the meeting. Yes, you will probably feel better after you have vented with this approach, but that's not the point, is it? Remember to focus on your desired outcome—improved employee performance. You want the employee to be successful. If you find yourself in a bad state of mind, it is better to take a short cooling-off period and delay the discussion temporarily until you can focus on the performance issues. Only when your state of mind is fully focused on helping the employee succeed is it time to initiate the discussion.

▶ **Respect the employee, but attack the performance issue.** Let your first set of words in the meeting focus on the performance issue, not the person. Managers violate this principle every day during performance discussions by using comments like, "Jan, you are going to have to raise the bar on your performance!" or "Bill, you have got to get your act together!" In such instances, the employee may feel attacked personally and will tend to respond defensively by overexcusing and overjustifying his or her actions. Notice the focus is on Jan or Bill—the person—in each of these comments, and also notice the lack of direct and specific language. Ask yourself what the person is *doing* or *not doing* and let that be the focus of your opening remarks. Try initiating a performance discussion in a respectful way, such as, "Robert, your sales are off by 32 percent for the first half of the month," or "Ellen, your store checklist has not been completed seven times in the last month." These statements are direct and specific and focus on the issue and not the person.

▶ **Take an "ask" approach and not a "tell" approach.** Once you make your opening statement, take an "ask-listen" approach by simply asking a question that will help uncover what is behind the performance issue. For example, "Tell me, what's happening?" or "What are your ideas for turning this around?" This approach will help you set the right climate for a problem-solving discussion to occur.

If you have the right intentions, if you focus on the performance issue by being specific, and if you ask rather than tell, you have the ingredients for a productive meeting that can resolve the performance issue. And most important, you have treated your employee with respect.

### Showing Respect by Communicating High Expectations

Managers who communicate high expectations to their employees show a tremendous amount of respect for them, for their abilities, and for what they can accomplish. Many managers, unfortunately, have developed the habit of communicating negative or low expectations, and, quite frankly, have become very proficient at it. In fact, they may be better at communicating negative expectations than they are at communicating positive ones.

> " Managers who communicate high expectations to their employees show a tremendous amount of respect for them, for their abilities, and for what they can accomplish. "

This happens because managers have "blind spots," meaning they communicate negative expectations and disrespect without ever intending to or even realizing they are doing so. This is typically due to a common personal trait to settle for lower expectations and therefore never be disappointed. While such a mindset may work for them personally, the result has the opposite effect on the people they lead. They are signaling disrespect, and they don't even know it.

Here are some effective ways to communicate high expectations to your employees while at the same time demonstrating respect for them, their abilities, and their potential accomplishments:

1. Set challenging targets for your employees and verbalize your confidence in their ability to hit these targets.

2. Listen—*really* listen—to employee input and feedback. Listening is one of the most talked about but least practiced skills in organizations. So listen for understanding. Ask questions and clarify what the employee is saying. Respect grows when people feel they are listened to.

3. Give plenty of feedback on performance, both positive and negative. Your recognition of a job well done is a powerful motivator for your employees. Use the communication principles in this chapter when giving negative feedback.

4. Disagree diplomatically. Here's a little technique I learned in conveying disagreement. Avoid using the words and phrases "but," "on the other hand," "however," and "though" when disagreeing with someone. They devalue what the other person has said by contradicting them. You don't need to contradict someone to offer another point of view. Simply say how you feel, think, or believe. If an employee wants to hire Campbell for a new position and you disagree, you might say, "I can see that you like Campbell. My concern with Campbell is his lack of experience in certain markets."

5. Be aware of how you communicate expectations and respect nonverbally. You want to be certain that your facial expression, body language, and tone of voice all communicate high expectations and respect to employees. If you unknowingly communicate negative expectations, you are apt to discourage your employees from delivering bad news, a practice you want to avoid.

6. Finally, communicate optimism to employees. Remember, optimism reflects your focus. You can focus on the best side of

people or the worst side of people. When you focus on the best side, however, you tend to bring better employee qualities to the surface.

If a manager demonstrates respect through communicating high expectations to his or her employees, their self-confidence will grow, their capabilities will expand, and they will achieve more than they would on their own.

Now that we've seen the role trust plays in effective management, we'll turn, in our next chapter, to the number-one obligation of all managers.

## Chapter Summary Points

1. Integrity must be a core value of every manager. Trust builds when employees see moral and ethical behavior in action and witness the honesty of their managers. Managers with integrity do the right thing even if no one is watching.
2. When everyone in a work group understands that honesty at all times is mandatory, trust develops, more work gets done, and results improve.
3. An open work environment in which employees can speak their minds and are obligated to dissent constructively is essential to building trust.
4. Always treat your employees respectfully.
5. Get results through your employees. Give clear direction, answer questions, make suggestions, and offer encouragement. Support your employees in every possible way *short of doing the work yourself*. When this support and empowerment is shown, mutual respect and trust grow.

6. When confronting performance issues, do so respectfully. Make sure you, as the manager, are in the proper state of mind. Focus on the performance issue, not the individual. Be direct, specific, and ready to listen.
7. Set high standards. Communicate high expectations. Demonstrate confidence.

## CHAPTER ACTION GUIDE

Ask yourself whether you think your employees would agree or disagree with the following statements about you, and think about them as you go through your day:

1. My manager talks straight with me and levels with me.
2. I get plenty of feedback from my manager—both positive and negative.
3. My manager is open and accessible to me.
4. I can express my real thoughts to my manager.
5. I can feel free to disagree with my manager.
6. My manager is very visible.
7. My manager treats me with respect.
8. My manager empowers me to make decisions and take actions.
9. My manager deals with performance issues in an effective way.
10. My manager demonstrates confidence in me and communicates high expectations for my performance.

## Chapter 3

# THE FIRST OBLIGATION OF A MANAGER: GET RESULTS

A ll managers know their job is to get results, but results mean different things to different managers. When I used the word "results" with my managers, I meant quantifiable and measurable outcomes from their actions that contributed

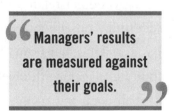

**Managers' results are measured against their goals.**

to the eventual achievement of companywide goals. I did not consider the number of e-mails received or sent, or the number of hours logged in the office, as results. Managers' results are measured against their goals.

I want to be clear that I view goals, objectives, and targets as one and the same thing. I'm familiar with companies that reserve the word "goals" for their strategic plan and the word "objectives" for their annual plans, but I believe it confuses people and provides too much wiggle room to not deliver results. This concept is too important to play word games with—and that's exactly what poor managers do. So to be as direct as possible, I would like to reiterate what I've always said: goals are the same as objectives and are the same as targets. Whatever you choose to call them, you need to get the results!

Typically, goals are initially established at an overall company, firm, or enterprise level by the board of directors, owners, partners, executive committee, or some other designated individual or group of individuals responsible for oversight. When I was the president of Verizon Wireless, my objectives were determined by a board of directors. I had specific and measurable revenue, customer growth, and profitability targets to reach. Further, I made sure the goals of all our employees related in some way to my own.

Goals of individual managers are established in concert with the manager's boss. Every employee's goals should relate directly, or at least indirectly, to his or her overall entity's. I suggest if a manager's objectives don't relate to the company's overall, then they are incorrect and, consequently, not worth obtaining. This may seem very basic, and it is, but I can't begin to tell you the number of times I have found managers with objectives in no way related to the overall goals of their company.

At the beginning of each year, I asked my managers to provide me with their goals, based on those that had been established for me by the board. I told my managers to keep their statement of objectives simple—typically, to just one page. When you approach goal setting this way, it is easy to eliminate the fluff and, instead, focus on those actions that will deliver quantifiable and measurable results.

Of course, the results managers are working to achieve depend upon their specific assignments. For example, the results sales managers work to achieve are different from those of accounting managers, production managers, or construction managers, but all their results should in some way relate and contribute toward improving the company overall. If managers' results do not relate and contribute to their company's success, they are doing the wrong things.

Now that we've established an understanding of what we mean by results, let's get into what we really need to focus on: *how to get them*.

## THE FOUR FUNDAMENTALS

We discussed the basics of the Four Fundamentals in the Introduction, but this concept is so integral to our management philosophy, it is necessary to detail it further here. Exceptional managers are able to consistently focus on getting basic, simple tasks done the right way, over and over again. They know the fundamentals, and they focus their attention on them. In the business world, the fundamentals supposedly vary from industry to industry, from company to company, and even within different organizations in the same company.

However, I suggest that only the following Four Fundamentals should be the focus of all managers. Everything a manager does should address, in some way, shape, or form, one or more of these fundamentals. Said another way, if a manager is doing something that does not relate to one or more of these fundamentals, he or she should stop doing it and start doing something that does:

▶ **Grow revenue.** Growing revenue is not just the job of the sales and marketing organization. Rather, all managers, regardless of their function or organization within the company, should work directly or indirectly to impact revenue. Managers grow revenue by selling and improving the products and services they already have. They improve products by offering new features and services for the products or even by packaging them differently. They also develop and acquire new products and services. For example, a service manager might implement a program to sell during a service call. A human resources manager might introduce an incentive compensation plan to stimulate sales. An engineering manager may roll out an enhancement to a product and facilitate a market launch in record time. Further, everyone in the company can talk to neighbors and friends about the great products and services the company offers.

▶ **Get new customers.** Typically, getting new customers is thought to be the sole job of the sales force, but this fundamental also applies to all managers within a company. Managers can directly or indirectly impact customer growth. For example, a manager in finance might ensure that inventory is ordered and shipped to the point of sales on time. A manager in information technology might provide a faster or simpler system to input sales orders. An attorney might find a way to simplify the customer contract or make an advertising disclosure clearer and more "customer-friendly." I think you get the idea: everyone can help in getting new customers.

▶ **Keep the customers you already have.** Keeping the customers you already have means keeping them happy. The best way to keep customers happy is to make sure every contact they have with your organization is a positive experience—whether they are placing an order, asking a question, reading a billing statement, or just seeing one of your advertisements. It's also easier to keep customers when they trust you. Trust comes from ensuring that your customers are receiving fair value when they spend their money on your products or services. Trust also comes from knowing your company is a good corporate citizen, obeying the rules and doing the right things. Once again, every manager in your company, directly or indirectly, can work to keep the customers you already have. For example, a customer service manager might ensure that customer calls are handled quickly and courteously. A finance manager might redesign customer bills to make them easier for customers to read and understand. A human resources manager could provide online training to emphasize how to retain customers.

▶ **Eliminate costs.** There are many obvious ways to eliminate costs. Some are harder to implement than others, however, because hidden costs can often become deeply ingrained in the way companies conduct business. The real challenge is to eliminate costs without negatively impacting the other three fundamentals. For example, all managers should focus on ways to do their jobs more efficiently. More efficiency means less cost. Speeding up or simplifying a process, eliminating unnecessary activities, getting rid of bureaucracy, and avoiding duplication are all ways to eliminate costs.

Remain focused on these straightforward fundamentals and you will enable your employees to align their daily activities and tasks with them, producing results.

## THE ACTIONS OF A BEST-PERFORMING MANAGER

The best-performing managers I've worked with appreciate that their role is to do much more than simply set goals for the people who work for them. They are totally focused on doing everything humanly and ethically possible to achieve results. All their energy goes into their efforts, and they are intimately involved in the "lives" of the organizations they manage, yet they do not perform their employees' work.

They get into the details, follow through, inspect, correct mistakes, and reinspect, all while never being distracted from their main objective: getting results. If obstacles arise, regardless of what they may be, they clear them out of the way. They don't just identify problems and use them for excuses; they solve them. They get out of their offices, roll up their sleeves, and drive progress—and they do so daily, weekly, monthly. They talk about results and post them where everyone can see them, and they have a contagiously positive attitude. Others like to be around them. Their employees respect them and want to do everything they can to help them get results.

Does it sound too good to be true? It's not. I've worked with managers just like them.

## RESULTS-FOCUSED MANAGERS DEMONSTRATE PASSION, OPTIMISM, AND ENTHUSIASM

On the way out of a "town-hall" meeting in one of Verizon Wireless's field offices, one of our employees stopped me and, pointing to the building's brick facade, said, "I'm ready to run through that wall for Jack."

He was referring to Jack Plating, who, when he retired, was the company's executive vice president and chief operating officer—the second-highest-ranking manager in Verizon Wireless. Jack's passion and enthusiasm for attacking an objective were contagious. There was nothing he didn't believe he could do, and as a result, his employees usually felt the same.

I first met Jack when Metro Mobile was acquired by Bell Atlantic. It was clear to me from the beginning that he was someone with potential to advance further in his career. What I saw was a high-energy guy totally focused on achieving results. Whenever I saw Jack or had conversations with him on the telephone, he always talked about his results: what he had done to hit his goals for the month, the week, or the day before; what he intended to do to make them even better in the future; which products were selling and which were not selling; what his competitors were doing and how he planned to beat them. You get the idea.

But Jack also did more than just talk about his results. He posted them on whiteboards in his stores, call centers, regional offices, and everywhere else he could for his employees to see so they could know exactly where they and their fellow employees stood in the quest to reach their goals. When he talked about his goals, he could break them down so the employees who worked for him understood their role in achieving the desired results. Jack was a proactive manager with a keen understanding that the ultimate goal of a successful manager is to have this total commitment spread throughout the entire organization at all levels so that a results-focused culture is created.

> The ultimate goal of a successful manager is to have this total commitment spread throughout the entire organization at all levels so that a results-focused culture is created.

Frank worked for another such manager, named Ken Lipke, who was the president and CEO of Gibraltar Steel. Like Jack, Ken, too, was a results-based manager, one who grew his company by leaps and bounds. He drove results through a personal belief that everything was possible, and he had an infectious enthusiasm that permeated his entire organization. If anyone in the Gibraltar plant or office asked him how he was doing, his response would always be the same: "Terrific!" he would exclaim (as opposed to managers who respond by saying, "Better than nothing," or "I'm here," or "Another day, another dollar"). Ken exuded optimism for everything he did. He lifted the energy level of everyone he came into contact with. Employees were greeted with a slogan of his upon arrival at work: *"Welcome to the World of Opportunity!"* It was a reminder that each day was an opportunity to get results for the company and the customer.

Whenever he had a strategic goal, like becoming a model supplier for a major automaker or growing revenue from $10 million to $100 million in 10 years, he attacked it with tenacity. His daily, weekly, monthly, and annual objectives all had to be aligned with the company's goal—any that were off target during the course of a year became a priority for realignment.

Ken would not accept general comments from managers such as, "We are going to redouble our efforts" as a response to a shortcoming or missed goal. He would instead respond with questions like, "How are you specifically redoubling your efforts?" or "What specific actions are you taking?" even if this produced an uncomfortable conversation. He wanted to get into the details of fixing the problem—the concrete plans, not glittering generalities. Ken would instill accountability in all those under him during every step of their day. Quarterly employee town-hall meetings became an opportunity to reinforce the importance of the goals and to provide feedback on progress toward them.

Like Ken, the most successful, results-driven managers I've worked with have always demonstrated these behaviors and characteristics routinely:

▶ A relentless, daily focus on achieving results and an adherence to concrete plans to do so

▶ A keen eye for opportunities on how to improve results in the future

▶ An understanding of what the competition is doing and how they can plan to beat the competition

▶ A commitment to translate their own goals to their employees by breaking down the goals into bite-size, attainable targets tailored for each employee

▶ The creative skill to apply visible reminders for people to know where they stand in relation to their planned objectives

▶ A commitment to driving goals through a contagious passion

▶ An unyielding belief that their targets can be reached

▶ A talent for lifting the energy level of people they work with

▶ An involvement in the critical details of achieving goals

▶ A skill for instilling accountability in goal achievement

There are, of course, those managers who don't consider achieving results to be their first order of business. In a results-focused environment, their negative characteristics stand out, and they fail to reach their goals. Typically, these managers:

▶ Frequently miss deadlines and goals

▶ Lack accountability in achieving results

▶ Have numerous excuses and rationalizations for not getting things done

▶ Retain employees who miss commitments to each other

▶ Lack attention to details

▶ Lack commitment to action plans

▶ Can't make decisions

▶ Don't have milestones in their plans

▶ Lack firm time commitments

▶ Lack formal monitoring of action plans

▶ Fail to take corrective action when goals are not being met

Managers like Jack and Ken strived to produce results, instilling the same goal-reaching values in their employees that they managed by. Their ability to energize their workforce supported the organization and pushed toward the planned objectives. Through their daily, weekly, monthly, and annual efforts, they displayed all the qualities that a manager needs to meet the number-one priority of achieving results.

## A TYPICAL WORKDAY IN THE LIFE OF RESULTS-DRIVEN MANAGERS

Throughout the entire day, effective managers are focused on driving results and are the force that keeps their teams focused toward this end. So just what does a typical workday in the life of one of our superheroes of the workplace look like?

### *Morning*

The best results-focused managers I've known come to work refreshed, focused, and ready to go. I'd like to be clear about this: when I say refreshed, I mean they have taken time the night before to relax, wind down, and think about and do things other than their work. Whenever managers told me about the long hours they worked, or the midnight oil they burned, or the weekend they spent at the office, I would tell them that I wasn't impressed and that I would prefer they worked fewer hours a week and accomplished more in less time.

When I say focused, I mean totally committed to giving everything they have to accomplishing their goals for the day, and when I say ready to go, I mean they should have started already.

The first thing most managers do when they arrive at their offices is fire up the computer to check their e-mail. This is a good way to begin the day: check final results from the previous day, close out any lingering business from the prior day, check on any new issues or problems that may require immediate attention, or simply answer a quick question from a coworker. It's also a good idea to take a handful of those e-mails and respond to them by phone or in person. E-mail can be an effective way to handle simple things quickly, but it's very dangerous to become preoccupied with it.

Furthermore, managing by e-mail is one of the least effective ways of managing. E-mail often creates misunderstanding and, with it, more e-mail and less results-focused work. How often have you received an e-mail and wondered what the sender was really trying to say, misinterpreted what was written, or perhaps even assumed a tone or an attitude the sender really hadn't intended? E-mail is too often used by managers in place of talking to coworkers in person or over the telephone. E-mail–addicted managers hide behind their screens and communicate poorly as a result. At its worst, a preoccupation with e-mail will lead to "e-mail jail," trapping managers in their offices doing nothing but answering or generating more e-mail.

After starting the day with a brief check of e-mail, I suggest managers get out of their offices. As I discussed in the last chapter, the worst place from which to manage is behind a desk. After all, the real work happens *out* of the manager's office, not *in* it. So get out and visit your employees. These managers make sure members of their team know the boss not only is at work but is completely focused on making things happen, getting things done, and achieving results. Good managers know it's important to make the "rounds," let people see them, and ask questions of their employees like, "How did it go for you yesterday?" "What are your goals for today?" "Anything I can help you with?"

It is important for employees to see their manager's high energy level, enthusiasm, helpful attitude, and focus on driving results. Imagine how much more effective it is for managers to be there, face-to-face and available for two-way conversation with employees, rather than sitting in their offices and banging out e-mails to them. An in-person visit is always better than 10 conference calls or 100 e-mails. If managers have team members who are not physically in the same location, telephone calls (rather than e-mails) to check in with them can be a suitable substitute until it's possible, not just convenient, to visit face-to-face.

After visiting with employees and establishing the tone and results focus for the day, it's time to deal with any pressing issues that may need to be resolved, or to catch up on reading and writing reports, returning telephone calls, or talking with customers and suppliers.

This is also an opportune time to attend meetings that have been scheduled. In regard to meetings, it's commonly understood that managers attend one after another all day long. Managers who do so, however, are usually ineffective. There will always be plenty of meetings for managers to attend. The challenge managers face, however, is to determine up front whether any given meeting will help them get results. If not, the meeting probably will be a waste of time. (You'll read more about this in Chapter 4.)

### Afternoon

Undoubtedly, the morning has gone fast, and it's now time for a quick lunch. I always found this to be a good time to reenergize and prepare myself for the afternoon. We all have our own way of doing it, but for me a few minutes of exercise or a brisk walk renewed my energy and gave me time to get mentally ready for the afternoon. On the other hand, "going out to lunch" was something that seldom worked for me. Lunch with suppliers, consultants, or even my coworkers seemed, more often than not, an energy drain and a waste of time. In fact, I can't think of anything good resulting from such lunches. Remember, when people invite you to lunch, they have an agenda that very likely is to get you to do something for them, not the other way around.

Immediately following lunch is a good time to once again quickly check e-mail, return phone calls, and concentrate on any new or lingering issues or problems that may be obstacles to achieving the goals for the day. It is important once again for managers to get out of their offices to observe work, meet with employees, and, in general, make sure operations are running smoothly. It's also a good time to show interest and concern in what team members are doing and assure there is a proper focus on getting work done to achieve results. I often used afternoons to visit regional offices, call centers, training classes, retail stores, and remote field locations. Incidentally, the way to learn the most when visiting a work location is to make a surprise visit. In other words, don't tell a lot of people prior to showing up at the location.

## End of the Day

The effective manager's day might end with a final check-in with his or her team members to complete any coaching of individual staff that may be required. The end of the day is also a good time to plan for the following day. By setting goals and making sure resources are in place the night before, you'll be better able to get off to a faster start the next day and set the right tone for your organization.

I always tried to end my workday before 6:00 p.m., believing my ability to make good decisions had significantly diminished, as had my energy, by then. I also avoided business dinners in the evening for exactly the same reasons I avoided business lunches.

## Hours Worked in a Day

It takes discipline to be a results-focused manager. Managers are typically surrounded by people who are not oriented the same way, and since it is easier to conform to the majority instead of blazing your own trail, managers may lose sight of their goals. Many managers I've worked with have gotten hung up on the long hours they put into their jobs, believing longer is better. They feel an odd sense of accomplishment if they are the last car out of the parking lot. However, the number of hours a manager works is of little importance and not worthy of a medal. Rather, what is most important is the work managers get done throughout the day. If managers operate with an "I'm here, I've got time, I'm in no rush" attitude, they are making a mistake. When managing others, to use an old phrase, "Time is of the essence." Wasting any amount of time distracts from achieving results.

> " The number of hours a manager works is of little importance and not worthy of a medal. Rather, what is most important is the work managers get done throughout the day. "

What about working at home during the evening and over the weekends? In my view, yes, there will be times when it is necessary to put in extra hours—but only for extraordinary projects or deadlines, which are the exception, not the rule. Will there be times when something has to be done at home to prepare for the next day? Of course, but too many managers arrive home, have dinner, and then crawl into their dens or studies every night and pound away at the keyboard, sending e-mails, or are glued to their BlackBerrys or smartphones even if they are spending time with their families and friends. In either case, I believe they are not allowing themselves the time necessary to get away from their work long enough to recharge their energy and renew their focus for their next day at work. (They may also be preventing the coworkers they are e-mailing from "recharging.")

## *Daily Discipline*

Let's acknowledge that what we've just provided as an outline of a manager's typical day is overly simplistic, and no two days for a results-focused manager will ever look alike. However, what this outline illustrates is the intensity, focus, and energy required by managers to get results. Results-focused managers have a daily discipline to avoid distractions that take them away from the real work of a manager. It takes discipline to avoid a meeting that might otherwise be nice to attend but not necessary for you to achieve your results. It also takes discipline to check your e-mail only during certain times of the day and not be distracted or lose your focus with the endless text messages you may receive.

I like what Nido Qubein, the president of High Point University, said about discipline: "At the end of the day, you are left with one of two pains—the pain of discipline or the pain of regret. Pick one!" He's right.

> ❝ **'At the end of the day, you are left with one of two pains— the pain of discipline or the pain of regret. Pick one!'** ❞

Without the necessary daily discipline to get results, a manager will fall short on his or her performance and will later regret it.

## THE ROLE OF DECISIVENESS IN ACHIEVING RESULTS

A core quality I look for in a manager is decisiveness—I want managers to make decisions and take action. I have yet to find a strong results-focused manager who was not decisive. When decisions need to be made, effective managers gather the facts, analyze the situation, consider alternatives, and decide on the best course of action—and they do it quickly! They don't procrastinate, and they certainly don't stand around wringing their hands. They move!

Further, once a decision is made, there is no looking back. The time for constructive dissent has passed. Instead, it is time for all members of the team to get behind the decision with 100 percent buy-in, even if their recommended course of action was not taken, and it is incumbent upon the manager to ensure this happens. Even the best decision can be undermined by lack of support and backroom second guessing.

Decisive managers understand that their decisions may not be perfect and, therefore, that modifications may be needed. They don't hesitate to modify or alter their decisions when it becomes clear that the original decision isn't working out exactly as planned. The effective manager knows that making a decision and taking action is almost always better than taking no action at all.

> **The effective manager knows that making a decision and taking action is almost always better than taking no action at all.**

Frank was conducting a leadership session in Toronto, Canada. It was a retreat for top-level managers. He asked the group about the outcomes of their decision making: "If you could go back through all the decisions you made in the last year, what percentage of those decisions would you make in exactly the same way?" The consensus of the group was about 50 percent. One participant said that even though he would change about 50 percent of his decisions in some way, he wouldn't want to get out of the "decision-making business."

Some managers postpone tough decisions with the rationale that they aren't hurting their organization if they wait until things look clearer and an obvious decision can be made. This rationalization couldn't be further from the truth. Many a manager has experienced missed opportunities resulting from this way of thinking. You need to gather facts and data, analyze them, consider alternatives, and move forward, making the best decision you can at the time with the information that is available.

I know that making decisions and taking action comes at a risk. After all, you may make a mistake. It has always been my preference to take the risk anyway. I've never considered making an honest mistake to be a career-interrupting event for myself or the people who have worked for me. However, making a mistake, realizing it, and not taking immediate action to correct it could very well be. Too often, ego and pride get in the way of taking corrective action, and the result is wasted time and energy.

The hardest decisions to make are usually the ones for which managers receive many different opinions on the best course of action. For some managers, myriad opinions would be reason not to decide at all. My advice to managers has always been to use their best judgment, choose a course of action, and get on with it. Furthermore, I always advise that if the decision proves not to be the right one, fix it as quickly as possible.

Have you ever had a manager who just couldn't make a decision? Unfortunately, there are many of them out there, and they are very frustrating to work for. As compared with consensus-building managers who procrastinate in making decisions, though they eventually will regardless of how late or watered down, here I'm referring to managers who just can't make a decision at all. Perhaps they lack self-confidence, believing they are unable to make the right decisions, so they take no action. These managers can be salvaged if they work for strong leaders who force decisions to be made.

Other managers might simply be lazy, or they don't want to take the time required to make good decisions. They are comfortable with the status quo and don't see, or choose not to see, that their decisions are necessary. These are the managers who usually can't be salvaged and need to find another line of work—one that does not involve managing people.

## *Decisive Managers*

A good example of a decisive manager's actions involved the multimillion-dollar overhaul of the entire wireless network system of PrimeCo Communications, a wireless cell phone provider in Chicago. Lowell McAdam, who at the time was president and CEO of PrimeCo, and the most decisive manager I know, wasted no time in making a difficult and expensive determination. PrimeCo originally deployed a network system manufactured by Motorola, headquartered right in Chicago. After a couple years of Motorola's providing PrimeCo with poor network service, Lowell decided it was necessary to change out the entire Motorola network system in favor of one from another manufacturer.

Prior to reaching his solution, he methodically gathered the facts, carefully evaluated the situation, and strongly considered several alternatives. He understood his solution could be fraught with career-threatening consequences if it turned out to be the wrong one. There were internal and external political consequences as well as expense and revenue considerations to be deliberated, and once the decision was made, there was no turning back. Nonetheless, he knew it had to be done.

When he asked the members of his board of directors to approve his decision, he found the board was split on whether to keep the Motorola system or switch to the other manufacturer. Time was of the essence, because without the new system, he knew his ability to keep his current customers and attract new ones was becoming more difficult with each passing day. He went to great lengths to prove to the board members who weren't in favor of making the change that his decision was the right thing to do. Through his own tenacity and perseverance, he won the entire board's support. In the end, he and his team of engineers successfully changed out the entire Chicago network system and put the company on a rapid customer growth trajectory.

Not all decisive actions are good ones. For many years, Bell Atlantic, one of the predecessor companies that later formed Verizon Wireless, heavily advertised the quality of its network service. Our advertising stressed the idea that customers who chose to buy from Bell Atlantic would have service in more places, less static, and fewer dropped calls than if they chose to buy their phones from another cellular company. The advertising worked for us. For years, we experienced excellent growth in new customers, and we lost very few of our existing customers to our competitors.

In the spring of 2000, coinciding with the launch of Verizon Wireless, we decided to change our advertising. We thought the Bell Atlantic advertising message was getting stale. After plenty of analysis from our marketing department and our advertising agency, we stopped advertising the quality of our network and began advertising what we called our "Join In" campaign. Simply explained, the concept behind Join In was to convince customers that if they bought their cell phones from the new Verizon Wireless, they were joining in something special. I was convinced at the time that moving away from our network-quality advertising and moving toward the new advertising platform was the right thing to do. The marketing team loved the new advertising, as did our advertising agency, and as did I, so we moved forward with our plan.

As it turned out, everybody but our customers loved it. For the next several quarters, our sales results tanked and the number of customers leaving us to buy from the competition spiked.

My decision to change our advertising was dead wrong. I should have known better. All the way back to the beginning of the cellular industry in 1984, I had been promoting the network-quality story. What customers want from their wireless company is to know that when they press the "send" button, calls will go through, and they will stay connected until they press the "end" button. Simple! My decision violated my own rule because I didn't stick to the fundamentals!

> **" When a manager makes a bad decision, he or she must admit it right away and correct it as swiftly as possible. "**

As soon as we realized that we made a mistake, we reversed the bad decision as quickly as we could. We went back to promoting the quality of the Verizon Wireless network with an advertising campaign we called "Test Man." You may recall the advertisements depicting a guy with horn-rimmed glasses, wearing a Verizon jacket, holding a phone to his ear and appearing in places all over the United States asking, "Can you hear me now?" This advertising campaign was extremely successful in helping us grow new customers and keep the customers we already had. It was an important and expensive lesson to learn: when a manager makes a bad decision, he or she must admit it right away and correct it as swiftly as possible.

Good, results-focused managers are decisive. They are confident in their own abilities to make good decisions. They are not afraid to take risks, and when they make mistakes, they admit them and quickly correct them. In our next chapter, we'll explore the value of simplicity in helping ensure that managers meet their goals.

## CHAPTER SUMMARY POINTS

1. Follow the Four Fundamentals: grow revenue, get new customers, keep the customers you already have, and eliminate costs.
2. Set quantifiable and measurable goals, and measure your results against those goals.
3. Make sure your goals relate directly, or at least indirectly, to your company's overall goals.
4. Focus all your energy on achieving results. Allow nothing to distract you. As the manager, you are the force that keeps your team focused on results.
5. Get out of your office to "drive" results. The real work happens out of the office, not in it.
6. Discuss results as often as you can. Post your results so your people can see them.
7. Don't put yourself in e-mail jail. Managing by e-mail is an ineffective way to manage.
8. Discipline yourself daily to get results and achieve your goals.

9. Be decisive. Don't be afraid to take a risk. If you make a mistake, admit it and quickly correct it.

## CHAPTER ACTION GUIDE

1. What are you doing, every single day, to drive results? What do you need to do that you are not currently doing to drive results?
2. How would you rate your passion, optimism, and enthusiasm as a manager?
   ▶ Very strong
   ▶ Inconsistent
   ▶ Weak
3. What steps can you take, on a daily basis, to convey passion, optimism, and enthusiasm to those who work for you?
4. Review the symptoms of a poor focus on results—the negative characteristics listed toward the beginning of this chapter. Which ones are evident in your workplace? Which symptoms need to be worked on immediately?
5. Do you arrive at your job refreshed and focused most of the time? What steps do you need to take to ensure that this happens?
6. Do people have to prod you to make a decision?
7. Look at the items on your desk or computer that are calling for a decision. Identify three steps for each decision that will start to move the decision-making process forward. Take the first step for each decision. Watch your momentum build.

Chapter 4

# KEEPING THINGS SIMPLE

**M**anagers must be able to clearly express ideas, suggestions, strategies, tactics, and plans; if you can't put your message in clear and concise terms, you cannot expect results to match your goals.

How many times have you ended up perplexed after reading a letter, an e-mail, a report, or maybe even a company policy or procedure? How often have you asked yourself, "What is this person trying to say?" Did you ever listen to a business presentation that was disorganized and cluttered? Have you heard yourself asking, "Where is he or she going with this?"

Often, these situations arise simply because people tend to use too many words to try to say what they mean, whether in speaking or writing. In school, many of us were conditioned to write an essay, a book report, a case study, or a term paper with a specific minimum number of words or pages. If you took a speech class, you may have been timed for the length of your speech to ensure that you went the necessary 5 or 10 minutes.

These past experiences may have taught us to focus on the *quantity* of the communication—the number of words or pages or the length of time speaking—rather than its quality. In this chapter, we would like to develop your skills in creating *quality* communications that are simple and easily understood.

Many years ago, a wise old boss of mine, Jack Clark, asked me to write him a letter about an idea I had shared with him to improve results in our telemarketing department. I needed to have the letter on his desk within a couple of days.

I was excited to have gotten his attention, and over the course of the next two days I worked almost nonstop on the assignment. What I wrote was a seven-page letter explaining my idea in excruciating detail. About 30 minutes after dropping the document off at his office, his assistant returned the letter. Scrawled across the top of it was a handwritten three-word note: "Net this out."

I didn't understand what he meant, so I went to see him for clarification. What he told me has remained with me ever since and has become a favorite phrase of mine. He said, "If you can't say it on one-half of one side of one sheet of paper, you haven't thought it through clearly enough to get anybody to understand it, and no one will take the time read it anyway."

Jack Clark was exactly right.

I heard an anecdote about the late, great American composer and conductor Leonard Bernstein. After a concert, an aspiring author approached him with an idea for a play. Bernstein replied, "Put the idea on the back of your business card and give it to me." The author replied, "I can't possibly put my whole idea on the back of a business card!" Bernstein answered, "Then you don't have much of an idea!"

The best advice I can give anyone about communicating in any form is to keep it simple. All too often, writers and presenters fail to get their messages understood because they say too much. The dictionary definition of *concise* is "expressing much in a few words." The best communicators are concise and therefore clearly explain themselves.

Sometimes managers fail to get their messages understood because they want to show how much they know about a topic and they want to further impress others with their vocabulary and the buzzwords they know. Good managers avoid this tendency.

So remember this communication catch-phrase: *One-half of one side of one sheet of paper!* This will always remind you to be simple, clear, and concise in all your communications—written and spoken. Less is best.

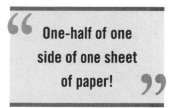

**One-half of one side of one sheet of paper!**

Now, I acknowledge that it's not always possible to write business material on one-half of one side of one sheet of paper. That's not the point. The real lesson here is to use this adage to simplify everything—memos, strategies, ideas, speeches, presentations, policies, reports, guidelines, and other communications of all sorts.

## BUZZWORDS: AN ENEMY OF SIMPLE AND CLEAR COMMUNICATION

Leaders need to communicate effectively so their employees know exactly what is meant and what is expected. They also need to be understood by large groups of people, both inside and outside the organization. It's important for their staffs to take actions and make decisions based on the focus of the organization. If the direction or focus is unclear or confusing, then the actions and decisions of employees will be uncoordinated and unaligned, contributing to mixed or poor results.

One aspect of communication that contributes to confusion is the use of buzzwords. Buzzwords are words and phrases that can have a variety of meanings—some wholly unintended or even contradictory to your intent—in the minds of listeners. From a communications standpoint, they are essentially meaningless.

Here are a few buzzwords and "buzz phrases" that annoy me:

▶ Spot-on                    ▶ Synergy
▶ Connect the dots           ▶ Paradigm shift
▶ Bubble up                  ▶ Ramp up
▶ Push the envelope          ▶ Traction
▶ Low-hanging fruit

Let's look at an example: you tell me that you are behind on an interdepartmental project, but you are going to "push the envelope" with everyone to get it done on time. What does that exactly mean? What specific actions are you going to take? How are you actually going to communicate the urgency of the situation, and what are your timelines? Specific details must be provided to even begin explaining how you are going to accomplish your goal.

So if buzzwords are essentially meaningless, why are they used?

Well, I suppose there are a few reasons. In the example above, it is much easier for a staff person to give a manager a general phrase like "push the envelope" than to provide accountability on specific actions, decisions, and timetables.

In many cases, people want to sound determined, even if they may have no idea of how they are going to get this project done on schedule. In other cases, these "impressive-sounding" phrases are ones they believe their manager expects to hear from a knowledgeable and confident employee.

## FOCUS AND MEASUREMENTS

Early in my career, I was transferred to Milwaukee, Wisconsin, to serve as general sales manager of Wisconsin Telephone. It was a time when competition was heating up in the U.S. telecommunications industry. Up until then, telephone companies were big, old, sleeping monopolies. They were also highly regulated, whereas their new competitors were completely free of government regulation.

I reported to Jim Howard, the president of Wisconsin Telephone. He was very clear about what he wanted me to do. He told me my job was to stop losing customers. He said he would support me in every way that he could, but he was adamant that I keep customers from defecting to the competition and win back some of the customers who had been previously lost.

During my first day on the job, I called my six district sales managers to a hastily prepared staff meeting. I told them I expected to start beating our competitors, keeping the customers we have, and winning back customers who had left us. They all looked at me, the new guy, as if I were from Mars.

I patiently listened to them for over an hour as they explained all the reasons why they were losing customers. Then I simply told them that from this point forward, no excuse for losing customers was acceptable. I concluded the meeting by telling each of them to meet with me individually the following day to discuss their district's objectives, results, and success, based on a going-forward plan.

The meetings the next day proved to be painful, each one unfolding in a similar way. The managers had very similar sets of clear objectives, and they were all meeting or exceeding their goals. However, their objectives were focused on the wrong results! They were related to making sales calls, conducting work reviews, avoiding motor vehicle accidents, maintaining good attendance, and other nice things to do. Needless to say, it wasn't hard for me to figure out why we were rapidly losing customers: *not one* of my managers was focused on retaining our customers. Their focus was off, and they were measuring their success based on criteria that did not meet the desired results.

I quickly established revenue growth and customer retention targets for each district manager. We tracked our results daily and discussed how to improve continuously. In addition, every district manager, sales manager, and sales representative attended intensive selling-skills and product training. Numerous programs were put into place to focus our employees and improve results. Several nonperforming managers were replaced.

As a result of our efforts, we started growing revenue and beating the competition within 6 months. Within 12 months, we were winning back customers from our competitors.

What made the difference? It all started with having the right focus and measuring the right criteria.

When you have the wrong focus, you create the wrong measurements. When you have the wrong measurements, you measure things that have no significant effect on the real results that matter.

Just one more point on focus and measurements: don't play games with the numbers! Frank had a telephone company client that measured "installations completed on time." If a new convenience store was being constructed, the phone company would agree to complete installation of lines by a certain date to coincide with the opening of the store. When Frank looked at the percentage of completed installations, they were close to 90 percent, a number management was proud of.

Unfortunately, after a short period of time, Frank found the flaw in the percentage. The phone company defined "installations completed on time" as any installation completed *within 30 days of the agreed-upon time.* The percentage lacked integrity. The real on-time completion number—the installations completed by the agreed-upon date—was closer to 60 percent. If you are serious about focus and measurements, you want to ensure that your numbers are real.

> ❝ **When you have the wrong focus, you create the wrong measurements. When you have the wrong measurements, you measure things that have no significant effect on the real results that matter.** ❞

### Simplicity and the Four Fundamentals

The concept of the Four Fundamentals goes hand-in-hand with keeping things simple: grow revenue, get new customers, keep the customers you already have, and eliminate costs. Concentrating on these four aspects, and these four aspects alone, will lead your success as a manager. The Leadership Focus Worksheet that follows may be useful for new managers or experienced managers who want to refresh their skills. Use the worksheet to identify your role and focus in applying each of the Four Fundamentals, and then identify other functions and how they can impact this focus, either directly or indirectly. When reading the rest of this chapter, keep the Four Fundamentals in mind.

*continued*

## Leadership Focus Worksheet

### Grow Revenue

How my function can impact this focus, either directly or indirectly.

How other functions can impact this focus, either directly or indirectly.

_____

_____

_____

_____

### Get New Customers

How my function can impact this focus, either directly or indirectly.

How other functions can impact this focus, either directly or indirectly.

_____

_____

_____

_____

### Keep the Customers You Already Have

How my function can impact this focus, either directly or indirectly.

How other functions can impact this focus, either directly or indirectly.

_____

_____

_____

_____

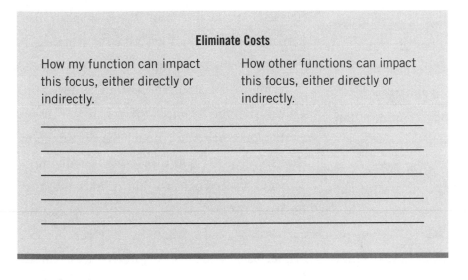

**Eliminate Costs**

How my function can impact this focus, either directly or indirectly.

How other functions can impact this focus, either directly or indirectly.

## KEEP THINGS SIMPLE FOR PERFORMANCE IMPROVEMENT

Achieving objectives is the primary responsibility of all managers. How many managers have you known who easily achieve their objectives one year and miss them the next? What happened to them? How did they get off track? I've seen this situation with quite a few managers, and most often it happens because they got off their game. They stopped focusing on the very fundamentals that helped them achieve their prior year's objectives. Instead of keeping things simple, they tried to do things differently and may have added complexity to their day-to-day operations. For example, instead of remaining focused on hitting daily sales quotas, pounding out one or two sales per day, they put all their eggs in one basket and tried to land one big sale at the end of the month—the one that never came through.

Good managers focus constantly on getting basic, simple tasks done the right way over and over again. Many sports analogies could

> 66 **Good managers focus constantly on getting basic, simple tasks done the right way over and over again.** 99

be used to make the point. My favorite is a basketball one: I have always asked our managers to focus on making simple layup shots instead of trying to sink hook shots from center court. Obviously, the chances of making a basic, simple layup are much better than making any shot from center court. It's undoubtedly more fun and spectacular to sink a three-pointer far from the top of the key, but why take the chance? When teams start losing games, what do their coaches do? They have the players practice basic drills in an effort to refocus on the fundamentals of the game.

There is another lesson here, too; it's one Frank learned from playing basketball at Canisius College under Coach Bob MacKinnon. He said Coach MacKinnon believed in mastering the fundamentals. The players did the same basic basketball drills—like boxing out, doing foot fakes and drives, and protecting the ball—for four straight years. Coach MacKinnon wanted each player to have the confidence that he was better at the fundamentals than his counterpart on the opposing team.

What is the lesson here? Canisius basketball developed a reputation as a "giant killer." Each season, the team was able to beat superior, ranked teams because the players mastered the fundamentals. In other words, a proven way to beat larger competitors is to beat them at the basics—this holds true in both basketball and business.

If you have a performance problem, identify the basics that are creating the problem. This is normally a three-step process, as follows:

1. **Identify what measurable factors need to be corrected.** Fundamental, measurable factors need to be corrected to solve a per-

formance problem. If a sales representative is not meeting a sales quota, it could be the number of calls, the number of appointments, or the number of sales that is causing the problem. If an engineer is not completing projects in a timely manner, the weekly requirements that lead to a completed project on time may be the obstacle. If a manufacturing manager is falling short on a production quota, the number of product defects could be the contributing factor. For a store manager, the measurable factors might include a clean store window, stocked shelves, and trained employees. In each case, a measurable factor needs to be identified.

2. **Identify what has to be done on a daily basis to correct the course.** The next step is to break the measurable factor down to a daily number that you have to achieve to bring your performance up to requirements. For example, a manufacturing manager might have to reduce product defects by 4 percent a day to hit his or her quarterly target.

3. **Identify the specific behaviors that need to be changed.** The final step is to focus on the specific behaviors that will help bring performance up to standards. This step involves your role as a coach. Is it making more sales calls? Is it changing a sales representative's prospecting message to get better results? Is it improving presentation skills on calls to close more sales? Is it a new short meeting at the beginning or end of a shift to measure defects on a daily basis? Is it a store manager using a daily checklist to ensure that store requirements are met?

A very common problem that managers have in improving an employee's behavior when there is a performance problem is this:

instead of using the simple three-step process just described, they use metaphors, generalities, and attitude to try to stimulate improvement. It almost never works.

The left column in the table below lists some of the statements that managers use in discussing performance issues. Instead of using these types of phrases, it is important to focus on the specific behavior that needs to be changed. In other words, what is the person *doing* or *not doing* that is creating the performance problem? If you ask that question, you will get to tangible, measurable, and specific behaviors—the first step toward a solution.

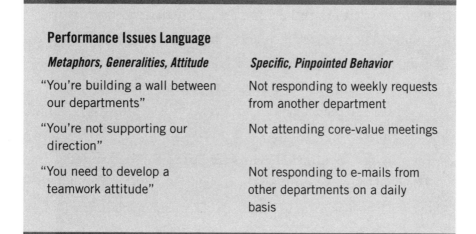

### Performance Issues Language

| Metaphors, Generalities, Attitude | Specific, Pinpointed Behavior |
| --- | --- |
| "You're building a wall between our departments" | Not responding to weekly requests from another department |
| "You're not supporting our direction" | Not attending core-value meetings |
| "You need to develop a teamwork attitude" | Not responding to e-mails from other departments on a daily basis |

## MEETINGS AND VERBAL COMMUNICATIONS

A specific challenge that many managers face is the inability to express their ideas clearly and succinctly in their daily meetings. Meetings come in many varieties, but for managers they are usually one-on-one meetings, group meetings, staff meetings, and "town hall" meetings.

## *The Basics*

I would like to start by making a few points about all meetings that should be obvious. Many managers, however, either are oblivious to these basics or willfully ignore them.

1. Meetings should have a beginning, a middle, and an end. Unfortunately, many meetings seem to drone on forever or end without a conclusion—which likely results in no one really knowing why they met in the first place or what they are supposed to do next.

2. Meetings should start at the beginning and conclude at the end. Many managers, however, actually start their meetings in the middle. When people attend a meeting, the first thing they should be told is why they are there, or the purpose of the meeting. They should also be told what they will be expected to know or, more important, do as a result of attending the meeting. When people know these points right at the start, they will find it much easier to focus and to begin thinking about how they will perform the task set forth. The questions they ask will also be more pertinent. At the end, managers should summarize the important points covered and reiterate what attendees are expected to do as a result of attending the meeting. Finally, the best managers I know ask each attendee to summarize what he or she will do and when he or she will do it.

3. Meetings should start and end on time. Period! No excuses! The meetings should have a preannounced—and strictly adhered to—starting and ending time. Not only is it the courteous thing to do (after all, everybody has work to perform and objectives to meet), but it also keeps attendees focused and forces presenters to use time efficiently.

4. Meetings should not be held simply for the purpose of meeting. And if there is no purpose to the meeting, it should be canceled. Some of the worst managers I've known have held meetings for the purpose of scheduling the time and place for the next meeting!

## When Presenting

We have all attended many meetings. It's easy to know the good ones from the bad when you are a participant but not as easy when you are a presenter. What I will discuss now applies to presenters in one-on-one, group, staff, and town hall meetings.

1. Too many managers start meetings talking about themselves. The meeting is not about you, the audience members are seldom interested in you, and they don't care how long you prepared, how challenging your job is, or how smart you are. The attendees will draw their own conclusions about each of these. Some presentation courses tell attendees to start with a humorous story, a human interest story, or some such nonsense. Save those for a presentation to the local chamber of commerce or Rotary club. When you present to coworkers, get to your point quickly. Even in one-on-one discussions, I've known managers to spend so much time talking pleasantries that there is little time left for substantive discussion. The best managers I've encountered don't spend any time talking about their own issues

> **The meeting is not about you, the audience members are seldom interested in you, and they don't care how long you prepared, how challenging your job is, or how smart you are.**

or problems or anything else about themselves; they get right to the point.

2. Imagine yourself as a member of the audience. Present only information the audience members need to know. You will not impress them by telling them everything you know about a subject. They don't want to know what *you* know. They want to know what *they* need to know or do. Anything more than that will cause them to look at their watches, read their e-mails, and generally lose interest. I've known audiences who have become so bored that they began texting each other for amusement.

3. Be prepared to talk without your PowerPoint presentation or stack of charts. The best presentations I've seen have been those in which the presenters put the charts aside and simply explained why they were presenting, what they would ask the audience to do when they were finished, and why they should do what they were being asked. This would be followed by a few minutes on the benefits, risks, costs, next steps, and a call to action. Your chances of delivering a successful presentation are inversely proportional to the size of your presentation. The larger the presentation, the more likely the failure. Please understand, I'm not suggesting that presenters don't need to be thorough; of course they do. But the best presenters are thorough while still remaining clear and concise.

When I attended meetings in which presenters intended to cover a large number of charts, after about five minutes, I would ask them to flip to the two or three charts in their pile that best made the points they believed the audience needed to know. I would then tell them to stick to those charts and ignore the rest.

This technique almost always led to better presentations in much less time than originally allocated. I suggest that any presentation can be made clearly and concisely with 10 or fewer charts.

4.  Conclude every presentation with an opportunity for members of the audience to ask any questions they haven't already asked, and if appropriate, be sure to provide the audience with a clear summary of action items and completion dates.

## *When Conducting*

At this point, it might be helpful to make a few suggestions to managers when they conduct meetings.

1.  This will be obvious: open meetings in a way that makes the participants feel welcome and comfortable. If you have any doubt that it is not already understood, let people know you are interested in their points of view. A couple of pleasantries are always appropriate to begin a meeting, but move quickly to the issues at hand.

2.  Be open to differences in opinion. Listen carefully. Learn the facts. Ask clarifying questions. Give clear advice. Ask if your advice is clear. At the end of the meetings, I would often ask individuals what they heard, what they will do next, and when they will do it. I also asked whether they got what they needed from me.

3.  Stay calm and even-tempered when disagreements arise. Avoid getting angry or raising your voice for any reason, and don't allow negative comments to get personal.

4.  Avoid lunch meetings—they are a waste of time. The travel time creates an inconvenience, and very little business can be conducted while reading a menu, waiting to place an order, waiting to be served, and trying to speak with a mouth full of food.

5. And bear in mind that nothing good ever happens at meetings over drinks or dinner. Avoid them both.

## Meaningless Commitments and Statements

One of the barriers in meetings is the tendency of people to make vague or meaningless commitments. The graphic below illustrates vague and meaningless language. It is a form of what I like to call "gobbledygook language."

### Gobbledygook (Meaningless Language)

Here is my suggestion for eliminating gobbledygook or other meaningless statements: don't make or accept commitments from others that are not time-based. You always want to ask the question, "By when?" when someone gives you a vague commitment. I do get resistance occasionally from managers on this concept. They will say to me, "How can I give you a definite time commitment when I may have to depend on three or four other departments for support?" "Fine," I reply. "Then instead of giving me a time commitment for a result, give me a time commitment for a progress report or status report."

## KEEP THINGS SIMPLE BY REDUCING BUREAUCRACY

I have always believed having too few people working for me was better than having too many. With too many people, I have found that work expands to fill up the workday. Most employees like to keep busy doing something, so if there isn't enough work to do, work is created: a new report, a new procedure, a new policy, or a different, more complex way of fulfilling assigned responsibilities will be created to fill up the time available—bureaucracy is born!

Most employees want to have something to do, so they "make work." When not busy, there also may be a tendency for some people to fill the time complaining and commiserating. They find imaginary things "wrong" with the organization and dwell on them. However, when I have had too few people working for me, they are more productive, feel better about themselves and their organization, and achieve better results. (By too few peo-

> " When I have had too few people working for me, they are more productive, feel better about themselves and their organization, and achieve better results. "

ple, I don't mean understaffed to the point of not being able to get the work done; understaffing creates a whole different set of issues.)

How do you know that bureaucracy exists in your organization? Check for these signs:

▶ Too many approvals required
▶ Slow decision making
▶ Too many steps in a process
▶ Unnecessary paperwork
▶ Too much waste—e.g., wasted time
▶ Staff members, without line authority, getting too powerful

When these factors are present, your organization becomes a lumbering, slow-moving unit, instead of the agile, fast-moving team desired. Here is an example of bureaucracy in action.

When I first arrived in Wisconsin, I had a staff of 15 people whose jobs were to prepare and send monthly reports to the corporate staff organization. They worked on numerous reports, some voluminous, covering such topics as employee absence results, employee time reporting, order-processing errors, and safety statistics. (Incidentally, none of the reports directly related to the Four Fundamentals.)

I wondered who had enough time to read all these reports. My staff assured me that they were not only read but consolidated into corporate binders that were then distributed monthly to every officer in the company. I couldn't imagine any officer finding the time to do anything with all these reports. To verify what my staff told me, I called the marketing vice president and the network vice president to ask what they do with the "results" binders they receive each month from the corporate staff group. The marketing vice president told me he didn't think he received any binders from anyone, and the network vice president said he knew someone sent him the binders every month, but he didn't have time to read them, so his assistant "filed them away somewhere."

The next month we conducted an experiment. We cut the number of reports we sent to the corporate staff in half and waited for someone to call to ask us to send the missing half. No one called. The following month, we didn't send any reports to the corporate staff. I received a call from the general staff manager asking me to submit our reports immediately. I politely told her I had neither the time nor the resources any longer to prepare the documents. She warned me she would have to report that I was "noncompliant." I never heard another word about it from anyone, and we redeployed 13 of my 15-person staff into sales and customer service positions.

Unless you take proactive steps to reduce bureaucracy, it will grow and flourish in your organization.

Now that we understand the importance of simplicity, let's shift our attention toward ways to instill accountability within your organization, the topic of our next chapter.

## Chapter Summary Points

1. Express yourself clearly and concisely at all times. Use the concept "one-half of one side of one sheet of paper!" as a reminder. This concept applies whether you are writing or speaking.

2. Avoid the use of buzzwords. Buzzwords lack specificity and can mean different things to different people.

3. The Four Fundamentals are *grow revenue*, *get new customers*, *keep the customers you already have*, and *eliminate costs*. If what you are

doing does not address one or more of these Four Fundamentals, examine why you are doing it.

4. Make sure you are measuring results that matter—those results that relate directly or indirectly to the Four Fundamentals above. Don't waste time measuring things that don't relate to the fundamentals.

5. Organize your meetings. Make sure every meeting you call has a purpose, starts and ends on time, and actually accomplishes what you set out to accomplish.

6. Focus your meeting presentation (either one-on-one or to an audience) on what the person or audience attending needs to know. Don't waste any time getting to the point. If necessary, be prepared to talk without your PowerPoint presentation and charts. Conclude every presentation with a summary, including action items.

## CHAPTER ACTION GUIDE

1. Take out a recent presentation you made. Using the principle of "one-half of one side of one sheet of paper," remove all buzzwords and material that does not contribute to simplicity.

2. Make a copy of the Leadership Focus Worksheet from earlier in this chapter. Keep it visible at your workplace. Review it every morning as a reminder of your focus for the day. Then review it in the evening before you leave to determine whether your activities and tasks that day contributed to the Four Fundamentals. Do this until you have automatically developed the habit of focusing on these fundamentals.

3. Review your daily schedule or calendar for the last two weeks. How much of your actual time did you spend on the Four Fundamentals?

4. Review all your reports that have measurable factors in them. Then identify each measurable factor by one of the Four Fundamentals. If you are having a problem identifying the fundamental, it may indicate that the report is unnecessary.

5. Plan for extra preparation time for your next meeting. Review the material on meetings and instill some of the techniques that were shared in this chapter.

6. Before you start putting material together for your next presentation, begin the process by finishing this sentence: "As a result of this presentation, I want the audience to know or do . . ." Then, test all your material to ensure that it contributes to this focus.

## Chapter 5

# THE LEADER MODELS ACCOUNTABILITY AND BUILDS IT IN OTHERS

A ccountability is the tool that enables managers to deliver results. As a manager, you assume the responsibility to meet your commitments and accomplish your goals. At the beginning of each year, each quarter, each month, or even each week, you commit to meeting these goals, and you are accountable for achieving them. Accountable managers do everything possible that can ethically be done to deliver on their commitments.

If you don't achieve these results, you have not fulfilled your responsibility to your organization. In this situation, good managers don't blame anybody but themselves. In my experience, I have all too often found that managers who do not achieve an objective try to shift the reason for failure somewhere else. It is too easy to say someone or something caused you not to meet your commitments.

Accountable managers accept the responsibility for missing a commitment and do everything possible to correct the situation as quickly as possible. When a manager is not accountable, commitments slide. Decisions don't get made. Responsibilities are not fulfilled. Worst of all, results are not delivered.

> " **Accountable managers do everything possible that can ethically be done to deliver on their commitments.** "

Why is accountability so important? Said simply, not much gets done until someone is accountable for doing it. I know this sounds basic, but it is critical to understand that accountability drives results. The best managers I've worked with not only assume accountability, but also know how to delegate accountability to the people who work for them. Remember, good managers don't confuse assuming accountability with not delegating: being accountable does not mean doing everything yourself.

## IF YOU TOUCH IT, YOU OWN IT

Before we move to some examples of accountability in action, I'd like to take a minute to talk about an accountability concept I call, "If you touch it, or it touches you, *you* own it." You will recall that in Chapter 1 we noted one of the reasons managers struggle is because they too often fix problems and not causes. A major reason for this is that often the cause of a problem lies in an area that is outside of their direct control. So what do accountable managers do when an issue not within their direct control is impacting their results?

> " **'If you touch it, or it touches you, *you* own it.'** "

Here's a real example.

A district manager of a Midwest customer call center, in reviewing her results from the previous day, learned that a large number of customers were hanging up their phones before being connected to a service representative.

If she were not an accountable manager, she might have let it slide. After all, her staff could easily handle the lower volume of calls, and they would have had more time to try to up-sell the customers whose calls did get answered. But instead of taking the easy way out, this district manager was determined to find out why this situation was occurring. She decided to first call the same 800 number her customers were calling to see if she could figure out why they were hanging up.

What she found was that the prompts customers heard (e.g., "Please dial one if you are calling to order new service, dial two if you are moving . . .") had been significantly expanded, most likely by someone in the headquarters staff organization. She realized that rather than listen to the great number of prompts, customers would get frustrated and give up before being connected with a representative. Attempting to get the situation fixed, she called the manager of the staff group, who told her the IT department had insisted the change be made. So she called her contact in IT, who said someone else was responsible. I think you get the idea: she was getting the runaround.

The bottom line is that after spending several hours trying to fix the situation, she convened a conference call with all parties involved, clearly explained the cause of the issue and the effect it had on customers, and insisted the problem be fixed right away. The very next morning, the old prompts were back in place, and call volumes were back to normal. She had "forced" the problem to get fixed.

The accountable manager in this example understood that even though responsibility for correcting the situation did not fall under her direct control, the problem was having a significant impact on customers and on her call center. The issue was "touching" her area of responsibility, so she took ownership of it and made sure it was fixed.

Unaccountable managers would probably have ignored the issue. When something goes wrong and "touches" them, their first reaction is to back away from the problem and find someone else to blame. Placing blame obviously won't solve the problem.

## Accountable and Unaccountable Managers

Accountable managers stand head and shoulders above others who shirk their responsibilities. Here is an example.

Soon after I assumed my position as president and chief operating officer of Verizon Communications, I decided to visit several business office locations around the country. (Business offices are staffed by representatives who receive all kinds of calls from customers, including billing complaints, new service requests, changes in service, and questions about products or services.) I wanted to see for myself exactly what our business office people were doing, determine how we might improve our results, and, in general, simply get a feel for accountability and productivity within these offices.

After visiting several locations, I was getting the impression that we could make big improvements in productivity. It troubled me that most offices were dark and somewhat dingy; lights were turned way down, walls needed painting, and old paper files were piled up on top of file cabinets and on the floors. In general, most offices looked sloppy. I also saw many people who seemed a bit lethargic—the energy that you would expect to find in a large office just wasn't there. When I talked to several of our managers and directors about what I was seeing, many of them said that the offices needed to be dark because the computer screens hurt the representatives' eyes; they didn't have the budget for painting, cleaning, and sprucing up; and such things were not high on their list of priorities anyway.

Then I visited an office in Garden City, Long Island. From the minute I opened the door, I could feel the positive energy. Lights were turned up, walls were freshly painted, and the place was bustling with activity. I immediately found the manager, who quickly waved me into her office even though she was busy on the telephone with a customer. When she finished speaking with the customer, she excitedly asked if she could show me her monthly results. Her office productivity and sales results were outstanding. I then asked how she got the office looking so bright and clean and why her representatives seemed to be so energetic.

She explained quite simply that she could never work in a dark and dreary office. I said I had been told that rooms needed to be dark; otherwise, computer screens would bother our employees' eyes. She said she had heard that too, but she didn't believe it. So she had done research and found it just wasn't true. She talked to the members of her team about the lights, and they all decided they would prefer to keep them on. Regarding the fresh paint on the walls, I asked how she was able to have her office painted when everyone else complained there wasn't any budget for it. She replied that there is always a way to get something done when you really want to do it.

I had found a manager who was totally accountable! How did she demonstrate it?

1. She took ownership of her office.
2. She assumed responsibility.
3. She made decisions.
4. She acted with a sense of urgency.
5. She took the extra steps necessary to solve the problems she faced.
6. She met her commitments.
7. She achieved superior results.
8. And, finally, she didn't complain or commiserate with others.

Undoubtedly, she modeled accountability, and it carried over to her employees, because her entire organization delivered superior results.

## Real-Life Example of an Unaccountable Manager

Now that we've seen what an accountable manager looks like, let's take a look from my personal experience at a manager who lacked accountability.

After reviewing results of the company's installation and maintenance facilities (these are the locations from which technicians are dispatched to install and repair telephone service), I decided to visit one of the worst-performing facilities to see whether I could determine why its results were so far behind those of other locations. This particular facility wasn't far from my office, so I jumped into the car and decided to make a surprise visit. (I found one of the best ways to learn what's really going on is to not let anyone know ahead of time that you are stopping by.)

The facility was situated in a residential neighborhood and included a large garage-type building and a fenced-in cable yard. As I approached, it was easy to see the place was an eyesore. The grass was uncut, and debris stuck to the fence. Upon entering the yard, I spotted broken-down, rusted trucks, discarded cable spools, overflowing garbage dumpsters, and cigarette butts and other trash on the ground. Two employees appeared to be just hanging around, not really working. I walked over to them, introduced myself, and asked who their manager was and where I might find him. One of them told me the manager was probably in his office and pointed me in the right direction. Before I left for the manager's office, I asked what their assignments were for the day. They told me, in so many words, that they didn't have much of anything to do.

Not surprisingly, the inside of the building was as messy as the outside. The floor was strewn with cigarette butts, candy bar wrappers, and coffee cups. Several of the lockers, which are provided to employees to store their gear, were filled with garbage. I found the unkempt manager in his office reading a newspaper. I introduced myself and asked, "Do you run this place?" He said that he sometimes runs some of it. By now it was obvious to me why this was one of the company's poorest-performing locations.

No one was accountable. Nonetheless, I asked him a few basic questions about why his results were so far off target. He whined that he wasn't getting the kind of support he needed from other departments, several trucks were broken down, some of his employees were difficult to control, and he was planning to retire soon anyway. I told him to go back to reading his paper, and I would take care of things for him. On the way out, I spotted a sport coat, shirt, and tie hanging behind his office door and asked why they were hanging there. He said they were there in case he needed them when the "big brass" paid a visit.

On the way back to my office, I called the group chief operating officer, told him what I had found, and asked him to give me his plan by the end of the day to fix the facility or close it down for good.

The facility was closed two weeks later, the manager retired, and the people and equipment were dispersed and reassigned to several other locations across the state of New Jersey.

Let's take a minute to summarize the findings of my visit to the installation and maintenance facility I just discussed. Here is how I saw a lack of accountability in this manager:

1. He blamed others.
2. He made excuses for his own poor results.
3. He whined.
4. He avoided solving problems.
5. He let things slide.

When this type of behavior infects the work organization, it is almost impossible to generate high performance. Instead, what occurs is lack of drive, low employee energy, lack of job satisfaction, lack of pride, and dismal results.

Incidentally, it's worth mentioning that this experience reinforced for our entire management team the importance of getting out of our offices to visit company locations. Everyone became more accountable!

If there is one key tipping point in the long-term success of any organization, it might very well reside in the accountability behaviors of managers and employees. Revenue targets depend on it. High-quality operations depend on it. Customer service depends on it. Quality products depend on it. Continuous improvement depends on it.

## An Accountability Self-Assessment

Complete the following Accountability Self-Check and the Accountability Profile Score Sheet. While this assessment is intended primarily for new managers, experienced managers may want to complete it just to see how well their skills stack up.

## Accounability Self-Check

For each of the situations below, distribute 5 points between two alternatives (a or b). Base your responses on how you perceive your existing behavior, not on how you think you should respond.

5 = to a very great extent; 4 = to a great extent; 3 = somewhat;
2 = to a small extent; 1 = to a very small extent

1a _____ I tend to rise above circumstances.

1b _____ I have a tendency to let circumstances get me down.

2a _____ I find myself frequently apologizing for missing commitments.

2b _____ I seldom miss commitments to others in the organization.

3a _____ I have a tendency to duck problems and issues that drop in my lap.

3b _____ I have a tendency to deal with problems and issues that drop in my lap.

4a _____ I tend to avoid situations and people that create discomfort for me.

4b _____ I tend to take the initiative in dealing with uncomfortable situations and people.

5a _____ I tend to have a quick "emotional trigger" and react poorly in stressful situations.

*continued*

5b _____ I tend to manage my emotions, which creates better reactions for me.

6a _____ I tend to have a habit of taking extra steps in dealing with job issues.

6b _____ I have a tendency to be in hot water because I failed to take extra steps.

7a _____ I have a tendency to openly admit mistakes, take responsibility, and accept blame.

7b _____ I have a tendency to look for excuses and rationalize my mistakes.

8a _____ I have a tendency to dwell on company issues I cannot control.

8b _____ I have a tendency to take the initiative with company issues that I can influence.

9a _____ I tend to lack follow-through on tasks, assignments, and projects.

9b _____ I have a tendency to stay on top of tasks, assignments, and projects.

10a _____ I have a tendency to let things slide and procrastinate on projects.

10b _____ I have a tendency to start on things and tackle tasks related to the project.

## Accountability Profile Score Sheet

| High Accountability | | Low Accountability | |
|---|---|---|---|
| 1a | _____ | 1b | _____ |
| 2b | _____ | 2a | _____ |
| 3b | _____ | 3a | _____ |
| 4b | _____ | 4a | _____ |
| 5b | _____ | 5a | _____ |
| 6a | _____ | 6b | _____ |

| | | | | |
|---|---|---|---|---|
| 7a | _____ | | 7b | _____ |
| 8b | _____ | | 8a | _____ |
| 9b | _____ | | 9a | _____ |
| 10b | _____ | | 10a | _____ |
| Total | _____ | | Total | _____ |

## Accountability Orientation Score

To compute your Accountability Orientation score, transfer your score
from the scoring sheet and subtract.

High Accountability Score        _____
               Minus
Low Accountability Score        _____

### *Accountability Orientation*       _____

Plot your Accountability Orientation on this scale:

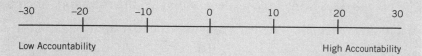

How did you score? If your Accountability Orientation score was 30
or higher, it is a sign of a strong accountability pattern.

If your score was lower than 30, do this evaluation. Review your
scores in the "Low Accountability" column. Check off any question in
this row for which you scored a 2 or higher. Each such question will
give you insight on where your improvement opportunities lie.

*continued*

For example, if you scored 2 or higher on question 6b, it will be important for you to focus on taking extra steps with your future tasks and projects. The higher your score, the more priority you should give to that particular area.

Note that managers who get results generally have a cluster of high-accountability behaviors. On the other hand, managers who struggle generally have a cluster of low-accountability behaviors.

## Accountability Isn't for Managers Only

Here's yet another real-life example. It's not only managers but also individual employees who can demonstrate high accountability, as Frank learned from an experience he had with an individual hotel employee.

Frank's consulting business keeps him on the road and, of course, in a lot of hotels. He is up early and uses the first hour or so of the day to catch up on e-mails and grab a light breakfast in his room. Early one particular morning, he heard a knock on his hotel room door, indicating his breakfast had arrived. He opened the door to find a young lady with a huge grin on her friendly face.

He said to her, "You seem like you are having a really good morning!" She said, "Oh, it's not just that, but I was smiling because you presented me with a big challenge."

"What did I do?" he asked.

She said, "You put out your menu on the door handle before 11:30 p.m., according to our instructions. However, you didn't tell us what time you wanted breakfast."

"So what did you do?" he asked.

She responded, "I called you several times, but there was no answer."

He was probably in the shower at the time, he thought. He asked, "What did you do next?" She went on to tell him that she went through all yesterday's menus to see what time he had ordered breakfast yesterday. Then she went out to the front desk to see what time he had scheduled his wake-up call.

She explained that she put the two pieces of information together and felt that this was the right time to deliver his breakfast.

Let's take a second to think about this situation. If she had simply called and Frank didn't answer, she would have had an excuse, or an "out," for not delivering his breakfast. If questioned, she could have said, "I called, but there was no answer." She would have protected herself from criticism. She would have avoided blame. But she would *not* have delivered a *result*—Frank's breakfast! Instead, she was the *cause* of a result. Through her proactive efforts to achieve a result, she demonstrated total accountability.

## How to Use the "Shadow of the Leader" to Build Accountability

Let's talk now about how accountable managers influence the people who work for them. I would like to go back for a second to the point I mentioned earlier in this chapter. The best managers I've met know how to delegate accountability to their staffs and, at the same time, remain accountable themselves. A manager must

> ❝ The best managers I've met know how to delegate accountability to their staffs and, at the same time, remain accountable themselves. ❞

model accountability and, therefore, by example, shows others how to be accountable.

One of the most effective tools a manager has to work with is the "shadow" he or she casts upon the organization or function. Many years ago, I attended a training program developed by the Senn-Delaney Leadership Consulting Group. During the session, Larry Senn discussed a leadership concept that was based on his doctoral thesis. It was called "shadow of the leader." It's a concept that has stuck with me ever since. I have used it in many management and executive meetings throughout my career. It never gets old.

People watch their leader very carefully. The *actions* taken by the leader, the *messages* sent by the leader, and the *attitudes* displayed by the leader all work together to shape the tone and culture for the entire organization. Like it or not, as the manager, you are in a fishbowl!

At this point we would like to focus on how the shadow of a leader affects the accountability behavior of the organization. Since this concept is pervasive, we will discuss it in future chapters with different applications as well.

The accountability behavior that the manager demonstrates has a great influence on the behavior of his or her staff members. Employees take their cues from the manager and reflect their manager's behavior.

Here is an example of a negative leadership shadow.

Early in my career, I was offered a promotion to a staff support position. After working as a salesman and a sales manager for five years, I thought it would be interesting to learn something different, and it might even open up additional opportunities for me sometime down the road. Without knowing much about what the new job would entail, I gladly accepted and couldn't wait to start in my new role.

Reporting to work early on my first day, I was full of energy and excitement, happy to have been promoted. After getting myself situated, I dropped by my boss's office to check in and see whether I could spend a couple of minutes with him to find out more about what I would specifically be doing there and to learn about his priorities and expectations. I introduced myself to his assistant and asked her to schedule me for a few minutes on the boss's calendar when it was convenient for him.

She told me he hadn't arrived at work yet and, therefore, would probably be running late for most of the day. I asked if he was available the next day. She told me she would let me know. Two days later, I was summoned to the boss's office. The meeting with him lasted about 10 minutes, during which time he told me he wasn't exactly sure what I would be doing, but he encouraged me to do my very best every day. He also said I should introduce myself to the head of our department, who would be in a better position to answer my questions. Needless to say, I began to wonder what I had gotten myself into!

After trying for several days to get an appointment with the head of the department, I happened to bump into him on an elevator. After introducing myself, I asked if I could meet with him. He assured me he would be happy to do so and told me to schedule time with his assistant. I responded saying that was exactly what I had been trying to do for days. He curtly dismissed me by telling me he was a busy man.

About a week later, after getting no direction from my immediate boss, I decided to camp outside the department head's office until he would see me. My strategy worked. His assistant finally rewarded my persistence with the honor of entering the big boss's office for a short meeting. Upon stepping in, I reintroduced myself and got right to the point.

I told him I had been in my new position two weeks, had done almost nothing in that time, and was still attempting to determine what, exactly, I was expected to do. I'll never forget his words. He said, "Your job is to carve out a niche for yourself and perfect it." He then told me I needed to understand that his department was nothing more than a cost center.

After a short time, I realized none of the other people in the department knew what they were supposed to do either. My coworkers spent most of their time complaining and commiserating.

Fortunately, after about six months, I was transferred out of the department. It was a bad experience, but I had learned an important lesson that stuck with me for the rest of my career. I learned that I would never be like that department head, would always try to treat people courteously, and would provide my employees with clear goals and direction.

What we see in this example is a high-level manager who has cast a negative shadow. He was inaccessible to people, arrogant, and condescending. In addition, he was either unwilling or unable to communicate clear objectives for his organization. What resulted were confused, unmotivated, and unaccountable employees—apparently, just like him.

## THE POWER OF "CRITICAL INCIDENTS"

A situation that calls for great awareness on the part of the manager is considered a "critical incident." A critical incident is a time of pressure, stress, or challenge for the manager. It usually involves a task, project, or responsibility. Often, negative emotions and fear are also associated with the critical incident, such as fear of failure, fear of embarrassment, fear of criticism, fear of loss, or fear of losing prestige.

Managers are often blind to the shadow they cast due to the anxiety experienced during a critical incident. They, however, send out messages loud and clear for others to see, hear, and imitate at such times, so they need to be acutely aware of their shadow when they are "under the gun."

We tell managers all the time, "What you do in a critical incident gives the members of your team permission to do exactly that, even when they are *not* in a critical incident!"

Highly aware managers will recognize when they are in a critical incident and will do the right things to cast a positive shadow at that time. Without this keen awareness, managers will risk setting a bad example and casting a negative shadow.

> ❝ 'What you do in a critical incident gives the members of your team permission to do exactly that, even when they are *not* in a critical incident!' ❞

In one of Frank's experiences, a manager was going to be criticized for missing a deadline on an important project. During the project meeting, she misrepresented data she had in her possession and actually changed some dates on e-mails sent to others in an effort to protect herself. Her staff knew it.

Her behavior in this critical incident cast a very poor leadership shadow on her team and taught the team that it is permissible to duck issues and cover your backside to protect yourself. (Once discovered, she was eventually terminated.)

Not all critical incidents that are handled poorly result in a termination. But nevertheless, they still cast a negative leadership shadow. They set poor leadership examples. Here are a few:

▶ A manager "throws someone under the bus" to protect himself or herself from blame in a meeting.

▶ A manager yells and screams about a deadline being missed.

▶ A manager becomes sarcastic when someone disagrees or has a different point of view.

▶ A manager creates false excuses for a report being late.

▶ A manager takes credit for someone else's work to look good in a meeting.

▶ A manager intentionally lies to cover up a delay in a project.

When a manager casts a leadership shadow that resembles any one of these examples, people in the organization see it almost immediately. It is hard, if not impossible, for the manager to fully recover.

Let me give you another example of a manager who had to work hard to cast a positive shadow even though he was under pressure to produce very strong results. I'm intimately familiar with this one, because the manager was me.

I was president and chief executive of Verizon Wireless at the time. It was January 2001, and we were in the process of setting our objectives for the year, such as revenues, profits, and number of new customers to be added throughout the year. I always believed it was important to set high, but achievable, goals.

The year 2001 was shaping up to be a difficult one for business in general and wireless companies in particular. (Some of you may recall that a recession had begun in Europe in 2000 and was beginning to extend into the United States by midyear 2001.) Customers were beginning to cut back on their cell phone services. Nonetheless, we were prepared to present our board of directors with a "stretch plan" for the year, and that's exactly what we did. During the board meeting, there was a lot of discussion about how difficult a year it was going to be for other divisions in the corporation and how it would be necessary for Verizon Wireless to make up for some of the shortcomings that were likely to result.

To make a long story short, we were handed some extremely difficult targets for the year—targets I knew we would likely not achieve. On top of that, one of our directors met with me after the meeting and insisted that we lay off people in order to reduce our costs beyond what we had planned and help ensure we make our profit target. This was very upsetting to me. We were experiencing huge growth in our company and would continue to do so, albeit at a slower pace, in 2001. We had never before reduced the size of our workforce, and we knew layoffs would demoralize our employees. Reluctantly, I agreed to both the new targets and the layoffs.

At the outset of this example, I said I had to work hard to cast a positive shadow. I was tempted to tell my senior management team that we couldn't possibly achieve the targets, that they were ridiculous, and that they really weren't my targets anyhow. Regarding the layoffs, I wanted to point a finger and say one of our crazy directors told me to do it. But I decided if I did any of the things mentioned, we wouldn't have any chance of making our targets.

So instead of grousing and commiserating, I accepted accountability. The unachievable targets became my targets. The demoralizing layoffs became my plan. Our senior team of managers, too, accepted our new objectives and immediately modified our plans to reflect what we needed to accomplish. Throughout the entire company, managers took on the challenge and accepted accountability. We all did our best to achieve our targets for 2001. The layoffs went as smoothly as could be expected and were even viewed by many managers as an opportunity to strengthen their teams and refocus priorities to the most critical needs of the business.

The bottom line was that at year-end the targets were not achieved, but we came close and, in fact, easily beat our own original plan in spite of the poor economic environment caused by the recession. We were proud of what we accomplished and learned we were even better than we thought. When we reduced the size of our workforce, we positioned the company for continued growth for the next several years.

If managers find themselves in situations like the one I found myself in, they have to make important decisions and difficult choices. The easy way out is to place blame on someone or something else. But to do so is to *not* accept accountability. It is also shortsighted. If the manager chooses to avoid and deflect accountability, there is little likelihood of getting the assigned task accomplished. If managers do accept accountability and take ownership for the task at hand, there is a much higher possibility of success.

> **If the manager chooses to avoid and deflect accountability, there is little likelihood of getting the assigned task accomplished.**

## How "Symbolic Acts" Set a Positive Example

A "symbolic act" is yet another tool for managers to send messages of high accountability to their employees while casting a positive leadership shadow.

What is a symbolic act for a manager? It generally has these characteristics:

▶ It is a decision or action the manager takes.
▶ It has real significance to the future direction of the organization.
▶ It is highly visible to the organization.

▶ It makes a clear point or reinforces a key organizational message—new or old.

Frank was once coaching a new president of a major organization. The previous leader and senior staff had taken a paternalistic approach to managing people, in which many of their organizational messages to employees were built around a parent-child–type relationship. The new president wanted to drop such an approach and develop a culture of personal accountability. Here is how he used a symbolic act to send a clear message of his intentions for change.

The new president discovered in his first few days on the job that the specially ventilated room set aside for smoking was very popular for employee gatherings during their workday breaks. In addition, he found that there were signs on the wall that felt like parent-to-child messages, for instance, "Keep your feet off the tables" and "Place all your wrappers in receptacles." These were not statements that had high expectations of personal responsibility!

So this is what he did. He went to the room during one of the busiest times of the day. He walked around and introduced himself and engaged in small talk with all the employees who were having their break. Just before he left, he removed all the signs from the walls and took them with him.

Within minutes, that symbolic act was the talk of the organization. He succeeded in taking an action that had real significance, was widely visible, and made a clear point.

And here is an example of a symbolic act from my experience.

When Verizon Wireless first introduced text messaging as a new product, few people found a need to use it. Even our employees were slow to catch on. In the early days of texting, I was often asked why anyone would want to send word messages over their phones. It just didn't seem to make a lot of sense, and customers were not buying into the service. A few months after text messaging was commercially introduced, I was beginning to think that Verizon had wasted a lot of money in developing the product and that perhaps it would never sell.

As I thought about what we might do to stimulate sales, it occurred to me that if our own employees weren't convinced that texting was something useful, there was little likelihood we were going to convince customers of its value. So I decided to try to convince our own employees that the product was a great one. I began by sending a text message to each of our vice presidents.

In the first message I sent, I simply asked each vice president to confirm that he or she had received my text message. No one responded! I followed up with a telephone call to each of them to ask why they hadn't responded to me. I also told them I would be using text messaging a lot, and I expected them to do the same.

Needless to say, the next time I sent a text message, every vice president quickly responded. I made it a point over the next several weeks to text each of them at least once a day, and I also began text-messaging other employees. Whenever I didn't get a response to one of my texts, I would call and, on occasion, even drop by someone's office to ask why he or she hadn't responded to me.

At every opportunity, I talked about the importance of text messaging. Whenever I spoke to groups of employees, I would ask the audience members who had sent at least one text message that day to please raise their hands. At first, only two or three hands would go up, but after a couple of months almost everyone, at every location where I spoke, would raise a hand.

Before long, there was a buzz throughout the company about our great new text messaging product, and our customers began signing up.

When employees know something is important to their manager, they catch on fast!

Not only did this example portray a symbolic act, but it also demonstrated the positive impact a manager's shadow can have on his or her organization. Clearly, the use of text messaging in the way described was a way to get people to start using it themselves and learning the convenience of it. When the boss text-messaged, it became highly visible to people in the organization. It showed the importance of text messaging as a new product that would be integral for future revenue growth.

Before we close out the chapter, here is one more symbolic act I had some fun with.

In 1992, shortly after we acquired Metro Mobile, I asked Rick Conrad, one of my very best and most trusted managers, to move to Phoenix and become president of our new Southwest region.

When Rick arrived on the scene, to neither his surprise nor mine, the region was in dire straits from a performance point of view. The region wasn't close to making its goals, and, of course, Rick's job was to quickly get things fixed.

At the very first operational review in August of that year, Rick told me that one of his largest customers, Salt River Project, a power company, had been lost to one of our competitors. When I asked why Salt River Project was lost, the answer was sketchy; I got the feeling no one really knew. Rick was never one to try to bluff me. He said, "Denny, it's gone. We shouldn't have lost it, but we did."

I immediately wrote on a single sheet of paper in big letters, "RICK CONRAD, SALT RIVER PROJECT, and GET IT BACK!" I held up the piece of paper for Rick and all his managers to see and told them I would put it on the corner of my desk and think about them every day until they won the customer back.

Every couple of weeks when Rick and I spoke, I would needle him about the fact that the sheet of paper was still on my desk. After about six months, I said, "Rick, this sheet of paper is starting to get discolored, and the corners are curling up." He responded, "I think about that piece of paper every day."

It was one week later that he walked into my office and reported he had won back Salt River Project. When he grabbed the sheet of paper off my desk, I could see that he was smiling. Clearly, being able to demonstrate to me that he had assumed accountability for fixing a problem that I had made one of his top priorities was something he could be proud of. Employees understand the significance of being held accountable, and they have every right to be proud when they achieve positive results for their boss through demonstrating their accountability. This was precisely what Rick Conrad had done for me.

In our next chapter, we will share some proven techniques and tools for building accountability within your organization.

## Chapter Summary Points

1. Accountability is one of the most effective tools you have as a manager.
2. When you are accountable, you assume full responsibility for the task at hand.
3. If you say you are going to do something, you must do it.
4. Don't accept excuses from yourself or others. Likewise, don't blame someone or something else for your lack of results. Accept responsibility.
5. The best way to get people who work for you to be accountable is to show them that you are accountable.

6. When you are in the midst of a critical incident, know you are being closely watched. What you do can reinforce and enhance your credibility and build accountability in your organization.

7. Likewise, what you do in a critical incident can also destroy your reputation with your staff.

## Chapter Action Guide

1. Have you placed a high value on accountability as a core behavior in your function or organization? Do you talk about it frequently? Do you write about it? Do you recognize and reward it?

2. Review the last few performance discussions you had with your employees. Turn back to the page on cycles of accountability. How many discussions with your employees were accountability-related?

3. Review the last few critical incidents that you experienced. Ask yourself four questions:
   ▶ What actions did I take during the incident?
   ▶ What messages did I send during the incident?
   ▶ What attitudes did I display during the incident?
   ▶ Were my behaviors something I want my employees to imitate?

4. If you were asked to describe your "shadow of a leader" in one paragraph, what would it say?

5. When you think of managers you have been exposed to, which of their symbolic acts had a big impact on you?

## Chapter 6

# ACCOUNTABILITY TECHNIQUES FOR DRIVING RESULTS

In the previous chapter, I made a case for the critical importance of accountability in achieving results. Behaviors and real-life examples were given to demonstrate both high and low accountability. You were shown how you can use the *shadow of the leader, critical incidents,* and *symbolic acts* to support and drive home accountability in action. In this chapter, I would like to take you one step further, by providing a variety of techniques to further instill high accountability in your workforce. These methods will allow you to reinforce accountable behavior daily and will help you lead your employees to achieving and surpassing their goals.

You will find techniques here that you may already be familiar with, and you can choose those that you feel will be most effective in your situation, but the main point of this chapter is to highlight the following two messages:

1. **Keep your accountability procedures simple.** As a manager, complexity will always work against you when your first obligation is to get results. You may find many of these techniques arduous, difficult, and time consuming, but they don't have to be that way. The majority of these procedures, which all use documents to one degree or another, can be created on one-half to one side of a single sheet of paper (recall the saying in Chapter 4). Make that brevity your goal. Your techniques will be clear and focused if kept as simple as possible. Your results can climb exponentially with an approach that embraces the notion that "less is more."

2. **Make these techniques important for the employee when you use them.** Every employee interaction a manager has is only as important as he or she makes it for the employee. For example, a manager can treat a performance appraisal as a task to complete and get out of the way as quickly as possible, or a manager can treat it as an important documentation process that shows the manager cares and is genuinely concerned about helping facilitate the growth of the employee. The principle I am trying to convey here is that *every employee event, experience, situation, and interaction is as important as you make it.*

> " Every employee interaction a manager has is only as important as he or she makes it for the employee. "

Consider an annual performance appraisal: it is not solely the task of reviewing an employee's performance over the past year that makes it important; it is also what the manager contributes to the conversation to demonstrate that he or she cares about the task and takes its significance seriously. When managers are thorough with the appraisal and show through their demeanor that they truly want to help their employees improve through the appraisal process, it *can* have a positive impact.

On the other hand, when managers show little preparation by swiping general phrases from other appraisals, when they hurry through the process, and when they are inaccurate with performance details or tardy with the appraisal, it will have a negative impact, communicating to the employees that it's not a high priority or it's of little significance. No matter how positive the feedback on the performance appraisal might be, the fact that it is presented in a slap-dash and half-hearted way will speak volumes about how the managers *really* feel about their employees. It also certainly won't reflect well on the managers.

To show your employees the importance of a performance appraisal, or any other accountability technique, keep in mind the following:

▶ Show the employee that you are *prepared.*
▶ Show the employee that you are *thorough.*
▶ Show the employee that you are *accurate.*
▶ *Communicate interest and importance* in your demeanor toward your employee.
▶ Be *timely* in responding to your employee.

Refer to these five points while you read the rest of the chapter to remind yourself of how to effectively use the following techniques in instilling accountability. And don't forget: keep it simple!

## EIGHT TECHNIQUES THAT INSTILL ACCOUNTABILITY

Let's start with two unconventional methods for enhancing account-ability in any organization: the first is the surprise visit, and the second is the unscheduled follow-up phone call. These accountability techniques are effective because they add an element of unpredictability to an otherwise typical day. In contrast, when conducting operations reviews, which are usually scheduled weeks in advance, employees have plenty of time to think about what to say and how to act and essentially prepare for the conversation. The day of the review arrives, presentations are made, feedback is received, the reviews end, and the next day things return to "normal." Performance reviews and most other accountability and performance enhancement techniques, too, are scheduled events. Employees know when these reviews are coming, and they have time to prepare. We usually don't think of doing things unexpectedly or spontaneously as a management technique, but I believe both are wise to help ensure that an accurate, real-life picture is taken of the level of accountability present in any organization.

### Technique Number 1: The Surprise Visit

Employees are not accustomed to seeing or hearing from their managers at unexpected times. In a surprise visit, the manager simply shows up at a store, call center, remote maintenance facility, or someone's office when the employee is not expecting it. That's when you really find out what's going on in your field locations.

Many times I have walked into a retail store to find the store manager, and sometimes the assistant manager as well, in the back office talking while the store was filled with customers out front, waiting for assistance. Needless to say, I was never too happy about a situation like that, and I would be sure to let the manager know it, but always in a respectful way. Before I would even leave the store, accounts of my visit would begin to spread like wildfire. Soon, every store manager began to think, "I wonder if he will show up *here* unannounced."

There is something about knowing that at all times you are expected to give your best that breeds a culture of accountability such that it soon becomes a way of life and the norm. This also ties in to our previous discussion of integrity and how we defined it as doing the right thing even when no one is looking. Working as if your boss could step through the door at any moment will always reflect a focused, dedicated effort.

> ❝ There is something about knowing that at all times you are expected to give your best that breeds a culture of accountability such that it soon becomes a way of life and the norm. ❞

Before I go any further, I want to make something very clear. Surprise visits are *not* an attempt to play a sick management game called "gotcha!" You're not snooping around in the hopes of finding your employees screwing up. Instead, your heartfelt motivation is that you'll be able to "catch them doing it right" and be able to commend them for their integrity and accountability.

The surprise visit is also a great technique that managers can use to roll up their sleeves and demonstrate to their employees what's important in the field. When you find something that needs correction, your visit becomes the start of corrective feedback. If you find something positive (like I did in the Long Island call center example in Chapter 5), it becomes an opportunity for recognition of a job well done.

In the previous chapter, I presented an example of a manager who was not accountable and of another one who was totally accountable.

I found both only when I made surprise visits to their work locations. To further clarify how a manager might use the surprise visit as an accountability technique, here is an example of its use to check on the implementation of a company policy.

At Verizon, we established a policy of cleaning up our building locations. The policy resulted from a few complaints I received from neighbors and municipalities threatening to levy fines if we didn't take action to improve the appearance of our facilities. The policy called for certain basics to be done, such as cutting the grass, painting the exterior, fixing any broken glass or other building components, picking up the trash—things you would expect to be taken care of in the normal course of business. But because of some cost cutting and, more to the point, lack of attention to detail and plain-old lethargy, these routine maintenance tasks just weren't always taking place.

A few weeks after implementing the policy, we visited several of our buildings located near our corporate headquarters and found most managers in most locations doing exactly what we had asked them to—cleaning up. I then decided to visit a few locations far from our headquarters to satisfy myself that our cleanup policy was being universally implemented around the country.

My first visit was to one of our buildings in Utica, New York. I chose Utica because it was a bit off the beaten path, and I knew that while the vice president in charge was a very strong manager, her office was on Long Island. I figured if she wasn't able to implement our cleanup policy in her "remote" locations, it was unlikely that her peers around the country would be able to implement it either.

My arrival in Utica was unexpected, as I hadn't informed anyone I was coming. What I found there was a building and surrounding property in shambles. In fact, I was told that city officials had visited the location a week earlier and threatened stiff fines if the lawn wasn't mowed and clutter wasn't removed from the parking lot by the end of the month. I asked the local manager, "Whose responsibility is it to clean the place up?" I was dumbfounded at his response: *he told me he didn't know!* After I made a few phone calls, the Utica building location was quickly cleaned up.

When managers make surprise visits, they may learn much more than they can by letting people know in advance they are stopping by. In the example I've just given, I'm sure if people knew I was coming to Utica, the place would have looked a lot different. My visit to Utica also sent a strong message to one of our best vice presidents that she needed to make sure she inspected her locations more often to ensure compliance with our policies. Unfortunately, simply telling employees to do something doesn't necessarily mean it will get done—particularly if they don't think you are serious.

### Technique Number 2: The Unexpected Follow-Up Phone Call

Another unconventional accountability technique I like is the unexpected follow-up phone call. During a meeting or an operations review, when one of my managers would mention something he or she was working on or a situation that needed attention, I would write a brief note to myself about what was said and put it in a follow-up file along with a reminder to call the manager a few weeks later.

When I would follow up with a telephone call to ask how the issue was progressing, I could often hear the surprise in the manager's voice on the other end of the line. Much of the surprise was no doubt from the simple recognition of the fact that I had listened to the concerns or plans, cared enough to call, and was holding the manager accountable. Once again, news of these calls spread quickly through the organization, and it became clear that the president may call at any time to follow up on what a manager had said and what was being done about it.

Here are a couple of hypothetical examples of how I recommend using the unexpected follow-up phone call.

In an operations review, a network manager tells me that a new cell phone tower will be constructed in September to improve service on Interstate 294 near Chicago's O'Hare Airport. In that case, I would write myself a note to call him in September and then would do so to check on the status of the project. Similarly, a sales manager talks to me about a new customer account she is working on. I would ask her when she expects to have the sale closed, make a note of what she says, and call her a day or two after the date she gave me to ask whether the sale had indeed gone through.

I would like to be clear about something here. What makes the two techniques we've just talked about so unconventional is not only that they are unannounced and unexpected but that my messages were not being filtered and perhaps changed in any way between me and the frontline employees. When I used these techniques, I intentionally did not follow the management hierarchy in the company. Rather, I used these methods to demonstrate to managers who were in positions of responsibility between the frontline employees and me that we were *all* accountable and needed to *do the right things all the time*. It was also my way of showing all employees that I was really interested in what they were doing, and if I encountered situations that were preventing them from reaching their goals, I would personally work to clear away any such obstacles. It showed employees that not only were they accountable, but I was too!

Again, I want to reiterate a point I made earlier. When you use these techniques, you will undoubtedly find problems, but you will also find many positive situations. Use the positive situations to thank employees, congratulate them for a job well done, and then share with others in your organization the best practices that you have discovered.

## Technique Number 3: Coaching

While Technique Numbers 1 and 2 are unconventional, Technique Number 3, coaching, is much more traditional and has a long and solid reputation for success. Let's do a quick overview of coaching, and then we will focus on instilling accountability during the coaching process.

The word "coach" comes from a French word that means "to transport a person from one place to another." In management, the role of a coach is to transport a person from one level of performance to another level of performance. If an employee regularly practices unaccountable behavior, the goal of your coaching effort should be to move the employee toward behavior that is consistently accountable.

Did you ever wonder why top performers in many fields have coaches? For example, professional athletes, singers, speakers, managers, and executives often have been known to have personal coaches, and the benefits of having one in those fields have become very clear. Coaches help performers by:

▶ Keeping them focused
▶ Giving them objective, helpful feedback
▶ Acting as a sounding board for new approaches
▶ Identifying blind spots that may be holding the performer back
▶ Reinforcing key values, principles, and behaviors that improve performance

▶ Recognizing positive behavior and performance

▶ Providing encouragement after setbacks and failures

▶ Setting "stretch" goals

▶ Acting as an accountability partner

Employees can realize these same benefits if their managers use the coaching process as part of their daily routine.

Despite the many benefits of coaching, however, a substantial amount of research shows many managers are mediocre or poor coaches. Some of the reasons they fall short include:

▶ They view coaching as babysitting.

▶ They see coaching as only correcting performance.

▶ They don't spend enough time with their employees.

▶ They are reluctant to criticize.

▶ They have social relationships with their employees.

▶ They have a "sink-or-swim" philosophy.

▶ Their coaching is not helpful or meaningful.

Though all these reasons contribute to poor coaching, the most prevalent is this: managers are busy and mistakenly believe that coaching takes huge amounts of time. This is not necessarily so. In fact, effective coaching may actually save time by preventing extensive retraining or intervention to get a failing employee or manager back on track or keep the person from falling off course in the first place.

Every conversation you have with an employee has the potential to be a coaching conversation, but it does not have to be lengthy. Short coaching conversations can have a big impact on employee accountability. It is how you use these short conversations with your employees that makes the difference.

The key concept here is to learn how to coach in small doses, which will help you keep coaching simple. You do not need marathon coaching sessions; instead, take advantage of brief, daily encounters with employees. Short five-minute coaching conversations with employees can bring significant increases in performance.

> ❝ **Short coaching conversations can have a big impact on employee accountability. It is how you use these short conversations with your employees that makes the difference.** ❞

Let's look at some examples of routine conversation topics you might have with employees where you can coach accountability:

▶ Whenever you set standards for performance or you set job expectations, urge the employee to take accountability for meeting the standard or expectation.

▶ Whenever you have a conversation about an employee going to training, cite the importance of taking accountability for implementing the new knowledge or skills on the job.

▶ Whenever you set goals for an employee, state how they can be reached if the employee takes accountability for them.

▶ Whenever you are delegating responsibility, urge the employee to take accountability for meeting that responsibility.

▶ Whenever you are providing feedback on negative performance, mention the role of accountability in correcting performance.

Obviously, there are many other conversations you can have with employees in which you can instill accountability as part of the conversation with them, but it is imperative to recognize that *every conversation you have with your employees is an opportunity to coach accountability*.

You must practice this technique until it becomes a positive, instinctive management habit and part of your daily routine.

## Technique Number 4: The 5:15 Report

One of the challenges of organizational life today is staying on top of responsibilities that are within your areas of accountability. It is easy for tasks to fall through the cracks. Many factors contribute to this challenge including:

▶ Travel schedules
▶ Virtual workforces, in which people work from home
▶ Employees who work at a different location than their manager
▶ Jam-packed schedules resulting from a strong sense of urgency to get things done
▶ The sheer quantity and pace of activities taking place during short periods of time

A simple reporting system, called the "5:15 Report," can give you a sense of confidence that you are knowledgeable about progress, issues, key events, and plans in your company, function, or department. The number of reports you get will depend on the direct reports that you have under you. If you have six supervisors reporting to you, you will get six reports. (A word of caution: your goal is to keep the report to one-half page and no more than one full page.)

The report gets its name from three factors:

1. The report should take no longer than 5 minutes for the manager to read.

2. The report should take the employee no longer than 15 minutes to prepare.

3. Usually, the report is due by 5:15 p.m. on a designated day.

Your specific situation will determine when the report is due. For example, some managers may need daily reports, but the information required in the report may not be available to their employees until 7:00 a.m. the next morning. In that case, the employee can do a report at 7:00 a.m. or shortly thereafter. Some reports may be due every day by 5:15 p.m. In many cases, though, it is done once a week and due on Friday by 5:15 p.m.

Employees have to be instructed very carefully on how to prepare the report; if they have to guess about the content, the intent of the report will be ruined. Some employees will want to put down everything they did during the reporting period, though the actual purpose of the 5:15 is to communicate vital information, not every activity. Here are examples of the types of information that you will find on effective 5:15 Reports:

▶ Progress on goals, plans, and projects

▶ Emerging long-term issues

▶ Emerging short-term problems

▶ Improvement ideas

▶ Accomplishments achieved

▶ Business opportunities to be taken advantage of

▶ Unexpected events

Here is an example of a 5:15 Report prepared by a department head for members of the board of commissioners for a utility. The items in parentheses refer to the type of information shared from the above list.

## Commissioners 5:15 Report

▶ Met with our engineering consultant to begin the planning process of waterline installation in the Tambury Estates (plan progress).

▶ Waterline improvements completed on Park Avenue (accomplishment).

▶ All regulatory water monitoring and testing completed on time by March 18 (accomplishment).

▶ Water leaks are causing overtime to increase by 5 percent over budget (emerging short-term problem).

▶ All goals and objectives for 2010 are on target as of March 25 (accomplishment).

▶ Water sales are projected below current budget by 8 percent for the first two months of the year (emerging short-term problem).

▶ We are trending down in water sales over the last four years ending in 2009 (emerging long-term issue).

▶ We have achieved the third milestone on time for the water plant basin project (progress on project).

▶ New radios installed on our 107 vehicles: communication problems resolved (accomplishment).

▶ Restructuring our bond debt now because favorable interest rates can save us $600,000 annually (business opportunity to be taken advantage of).

▶ We have closed the books for April and report a profit of $657,000 for the month, which is 7 percent above budget (accomplishment).

▶ The severe overnight electrical storm on March 18 knocked out power at our Erie Plant, but the temporary generator went into service preventing any water shortage throughout our service area (unexpected event).

Having this key information is incredibly valuable for making decisions, correcting course, adjusting plans, and creating initiatives. It helps each board member keep tabs on the business.

Here is what a 5:15 Report from a call center director to the vice president of customer service might look like:

### A Call Center Director's 5:15 Report

▶ Good improvement in handling call volumes this week: 90 percent of all calls into the center were answered within 30 seconds.

▶ Three new reps completed training this week. Staffing levels at 100 percent, effective Monday morning.

▶ Expense budget running slightly over plan due to overtime requirements. Expect to be back on plan by the end of next week. Will keep you advised.

▶ Absentee rate for the week was 1.25 percent, 0.75 percent below monthly goal of 2 percent.

▶ Sales volumes were $45K (below $50K goal). All product promotion goals were met. Volume improvement plan already in place with managers (will provide details on your staff call Monday morning).

▶ No system outages this week.

▶ Continue to forecast all goals for the month will be met.

Notice the valuable information that you receive in a short period of time. Again, as a reminder, your goal is to keep the report to one-half page and certainly no longer than one page. You can also use the report as a springboard to make notes and suggestions and return it as a reply to the department head. Similarly, you can use a reply to the report as a way to extend congratulations.

## *Technique Number 5: The Performance Agreement*

The performance agreement is a method for documenting what a manager and an employee, or direct report, agree the employee will accomplish over a specific period of time. This document is truly an "agreement," or a contract, between the manager and the employee covering what an employee is expected to do in his or her position. It provides a simple, clear, and concise means for employees to know what their boss considers important and what is expected of them. To this extent, it can be thought of as a contract for accountability.

Performance agreements should provide specific goals, milestones, and dates. The more specificity provided, the better the agreement. For example, as president of Verizon, my 2009 performance agreement called for attainment of distinct financial and earnings-per-share goals for the year. Further, I agreed to an exact revenue growth number, concrete customer service indices, and network performance numbers. In addition, my performance agreement included a few "soft," or non-numeric, goals, like "Strengthen our culture" and "Lead by example."

A performance agreement can be written by an employee at any level within an organization. For example, a representative in a call center may have a performance agreement that includes the number of calls he or she will handle each day, the number of calls that may be handled in which a customer's problem was not able to be resolved, the number of calls resulting in a sale, and so on. I think you get the idea: specific goals need to be agreed upon.

I have found the performance agreement to be a useful tool to document an individual's goals for the year. Some managers find it more useful to establish performance agreements for a shorter period of time—e.g., a quarter or half a year. Regardless of the period of time,

I believe it is important to update the agreement as often as necessary to take into account factors outside an employee's control, such as changing market conditions and new corporate requirements, which may necessitate a recalibration of an employee's goals. The performance agreement also provides a useful method for managers in initiating a discussion with their employees to evaluate their performance in meeting the agreed-upon goals.

If properly prepared, a performance agreement can be written in considerably less space than one sheet of paper. Measurable goals that are very specific often don't require a lot of words.

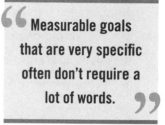

"Measurable goals that are very specific often don't require a lot of words."

## Technique Number 6: The Operations Review

An operations review provides senior managers with an in-depth look at the functions within an organization, the performances of the managers of those functions, the results the managers have recently achieved, and the plans they have to reach their goals in the future. The operations review also provides an opportunity to analyze the strengths and weaknesses of an organization and formulate a plan to improve its performance. Similar to the performance agreement, this review is a foundation for accountability within an organization.

When I was president of Verizon Wireless, operations reviews were conducted with each of our four geographic areas once every three months. Each geographic area, run by an area president, consisted of five or six regions. A regional president ran each region. For example, the Northeast area consisted of New England, New York, Philadelphia/Tri-State, Washington/Baltimore, and Upstate New York.

Each of the four geographic areas operated similar to a stand-alone business but with strong ties to a headquarters providing oversight and strategic direction. Each area had its own financial, legal, network, customer service, human resources, information technology, and sales and marketing functions.

Here is the typical agenda of an area operations review:

▶ Detailed presentations of the area's financial results and forecasts
▶ Marketing plans, including advertising, promotions, pricing plans, and competitive analysis
▶ Network performance statistics and capital spending plans and results
▶ Customer call center plans and results
▶ Human resources hiring, firing, training, employee promotion, and diversity results

In addition, each regional president presented detailed results, forecasts, and competitive activities for his or her individual region.

Approximately 20 to 25 people participated in the area reviews, and it was mandatory that each of the people who reported directly to me attended every one of them. We rotated locations where the reviews were held—usually a regional office or a call center—but never held them at the company's headquarters location. By conducting the reviews in field locations, we were able to show our employees their importance and the critical role they played in achieving the overall goals of our company.

The reviews were designed to keep top managers focused on being accountable for producing results and reaching goals. When we found problems, as we often did, the reviews also provided an immediate opportunity to take any remedial steps required or define areas for further analysis and follow-up activities. Perhaps the most important task the operations reviews accomplished was getting the managers, who were presenting in the reviews, to prepare by analyzing their own results, identifying where they were falling short, and creating plans to fix any lagging results and other issues. The reviews also provided an opportunity to share best practices from other areas and regions across the entire company.

The fact that all the top officers in the company attended all the reviews accentuated the importance and the seriousness of the reviews. It also afforded managers an opportunity to see that the most senior managers in the company were accountable for working together to achieve the company's overall goals, as well as helping area and regional managers attain their goals. It is important to note that since the top officers of the company made the effort to get out of their offices and see, firsthand, the challenges and opportunities our field forces were experiencing, it helped build a culture of accountability and teamwork throughout the company.

Traveling to the regional offices and call centers also presented an opportunity to hold town-hall–type employee meetings with large groups of employees after each operations review. The town hall meetings were a great way to talk about what we saw in the review and give an overview of how the company was performing in meeting its goals for the year. Every town-hall meeting ended with an opportunity for employees to address questions to me or to any of the top managers of the company.

## Technique Number 7: The Performance Appraisal

Much has been written in textbooks and management books on how to go about preparing an appraisal of an employee's performance. Many companies train managers on how to write and conduct performance appraisals. Nonetheless, for many managers, appraisals are one of their least effective management tools.

Why?

Because many managers consider performance appraisals to be little more than a bureaucratic requirement of the human resources department—often little more than an HR form to be filled out annually by managers for each of their employees.

Yet how can any organization expect its employees to be accountable for their performance if little or no effort is made to provide a regular, quality appraisal of that performance? I believe appraisals can be an effective procedure to assist managers in coaching their employees to higher levels of performance and ensuring their accountability. In my opinion, a performance appraisal is nothing more than an organized means to let an employee know what you, the manager, are thinking about the employee's performance and what he or she can do to improve it in the future. The performance appraisal is a written document that should include no more than three clear and concise paragraphs (in keeping with our theme of keeping things simple) on the following topics:

> " Yet how can any organization expect its employees to be accountable for their performance if little or no effort is made to provide a regular, quality appraisal of that performance? "

1. The goals the employee has met or exceeded
2. The goals the employee has not met
3. The manager's recommendations concerning what the employee should do to meet his or her goals

*The manager should write the appraisal.* I say this because I have known instances in which managers have asked employees to write their own appraisals. They then give them to their managers, who tweak a few words here and there and consider their "obligation" to appraise their employees met. Needless to say, managers who do what I've just described are most often not only ineffective but also lazy!

Another bad habit I've found with the way managers write performance appraisals is what I call the "cut-and-paste" syndrome. These are managers who take the exact words or phrases from an appraisal they wrote about one of their employees and use them in another employee's appraisal. I even heard of one instance in which the manager failed to change the gender in the cut and paste!

Effective managers carefully think about how each of their employees is performing and how each can improve. They then capture their thoughts on paper to review with the employee to ensure clear understanding and facilitate any improvement required.

Many companies require performance appraisals be prepared at least once a year and link them to an employee's salary or bonus pay. I suggest appraisals be done at least annually, but I think they can also be completed semiannually or quarterly. Regardless of how often appraisals are prepared, they can be an effective tool, used in conjunction with performance agreements, to clearly communicate with employees about their managers' expectations and the employees' performance in meeting them.

And if properly prepared, a performance appraisal can be written in considerably less space than one full sheet of paper.

## Technique Number 8: The Performance Improvement Plan

What do you do if an employee fails to consistently meet standards and targets? First, thought and consideration should be given to increasing the level of your coaching conversations to correct the performance. Or perhaps you may find that the employee is lacking a critical skill or knowledge that is hampering his or her results. You may decide that informal or formal training can be used to correct the performance.

But despite your best efforts, there may be times when you have to formally demonstrate the seriousness of the performance problem with a written document: the performance improvement plan. A performance improvement plan clarifies issues the employee is encountering or goals that he or she is missing and sets up a course of action for improvement.

Those managers whom I referred to earlier in the book who tend to befriend colleagues or employees and try to "be popular" will probably put up with a lack of employee performance rather than deal with it effectively. They will make excuses for the employee or rationalize the employee's poor performance. In some cases, they will even cover up the poor performance to avoid addressing the issue. As a result, these managers are doing a disservice to the employee, the company, and themselves.

For many employees, it becomes a "splash of cold water" when they are placed on a performance improvement plan. They are awakened to the seriousness of their performance deficiency.

A solid performance improvement plan contains the following elements:

- ▶ The manager's intent is to genuinely help the employee succeed.
- ▶ The manager uses performance improvement plans on a fair and consistent basis with all employees.
- ▶ There is a time period for the plan—usually 30, 60, or 90 days.
- ▶ The manager reviews the specific and measurable job expectations with the employee.

▶ The manager reviews where the expectation is falling short.

▶ The manager states what the measurable performance needs to be to meet standards.

▶ The manager states how he or she will support the employee during the process.

▶ The manager and employee establish progress review dates during the time period of the plan.

In keeping with our "keep it simple" concept, an effective performance improvement plan can be prepared on less than one full sheet of paper.

What are the possible outcomes if the employee does not meet the expectations of the plan? If the employee has made substantial progress, you may want to extend the plan for a short period of time. However, take caution here: if you continually extend the performance improvement plan, it reduces its effectiveness. I have seen "final" plans, "final, final" plans, the "really final plan," and the "last-chance plan," all, in the end, serving to make a mockery of the process.

Your intent and hope, of course, is that the employee will improve. However, if the employee does not meet the expectations of the plan or the extended plan, the manager should be prepared to take action. This may include a transfer or reassignment, a demotion, or a termination.

## A SIMPLE, BUT POWERFUL PERFORMANCE MANAGEMENT PLAN

When you combine the accountability techniques in this chapter, you create a highly effective and simple process for managing the performance of your employees in your department, function, or company.

First, you set the expectation of your employees with a *performance agreement.* Second, you have concise *coaching conversations* throughout the year to instill performance. Third, you use a *performance appraisal* to evaluate the level of employee performance. Finally, you use a *performance improvement plan* to correct subpar performance.

In our next chapter, we'll explore how managers' thought processes and perspectives affect the results they achieve.

## CHAPTER SUMMARY POINTS

1. Accountability techniques can reinforce the role, value, and importance of accountability in achieving results.
2. Keep your accountability techniques simple.
3. When you use accountability techniques, they are only as important as you make them with the employee.
4. You enhance the importance of any technique through preparation, thoroughness, timeliness, accuracy, and demeanor.
5. A *surprise visit* sends a powerful message, to employees and managers alike, of performance that is expected in the field.
6. The *unexpected phone call* to an employee is a technique that can demonstrate concern about progress with an issue or plan, it can hold an employee accountable for commitments and promises, and it can also congratulate an employee for an event or achievement.
7. *Coaching* can be extremely effective if it is done in conjunction with the numerous daily conversations you have with your employees.
8. *5:15 Reports* keep a manager informed on performance that is happening in the field.

9. A *performance agreement* is a simple, clear, and concise way of setting employee goals and expectations for a designated period of time.

10. The *operations review* provides a scheduled, structured, in-depth look at the performance of a function or department.

11. The *performance appraisal* documents the achievements and shortfalls of an employee's performance with recommendations for improvement.

12. The performance improvement plan specifies a course of action for improving an employee's performance.

## CHAPTER ACTION GUIDE

1. Do you have the techniques in place to make accountability a core value in your workplace?

2. Review the accountability techniques you currently have in place and ask yourself, "How can I simplify them?"

3. Review the last few performance appraisals that you conducted. Respond to these questions to help you determine how important you made the appraisal to the employee:

   ▶ Did you fully prepare?

   ▶ Were you thorough?

   ▶ Was the information you presented accurate?

   ▶ Did you communicate interest and importance?

   ▶ Was the appraisal completed in a timely fashion?

## Chapter 7

# THE MINDSET OF SUCCESSFUL MANAGERS

T he mindset of managers plays a crucial role in the results they deliver and the success they achieve. Every manager's actions and behaviors reflect this mindset.

When hurricane Katrina struck the Gulf Coast in 2005, like so many other companies, Verizon Wireless had stores and employees in harm's way. With advanced warning of the storm and time to prepare, we notified our employees when we would be shutting down operations so they could tend to their personal business and heed evacuation orders if directed to do so. We committed that we would communicate when it was time to return to work, but several managers took matters into their own hands.

Understanding the critical need for our service, many of our network managers risked injury—or worse—to tend to our damaged network. At the same time, store managers returned to "their stores" to get emergency phones ready for those who needed them. This action by a handful of our managers was not ordered by top management, and was even discouraged by concerned human resources managers; yet it happened. These managers understood their vital leadership role in an event like this and recognized that the company's, and their own, reputation would be affected one way or another. We had several managers working around the clock during this time under the enormous burden of knowing that their own homes were severely damaged or destroyed in the storm.

I remember the feeling of pride within the company as these managers' stories became known and my own personal pride that I still have today for these extraordinary people. Not coincidentally, these managers were also some of the company's best performers in their ordinary day jobs.

This example is an extraordinary one, but it illustrates how managers' mindsets play a crucial role in the results they deliver and the success they achieve. The most successful, results-focused managers I've worked with have a different mindset than that of the average manager, and these managers who weathered Katrina exemplify it best.

In this chapter, we are going to look at some of the mindsets that contribute significantly to a manager's success and establish the foundation for peak performance.

## THE NINE WAYS OF THINKING OF A SUCCESSFUL MANAGER

In defining managers' mindsets, I consider the following attributes:

▶ How they see things, or their perspectives on their world
▶ What they believe in or what's important to them

▶ Their attitude or outlook toward the people and setting around them

▶ Their views and pattern of thinking

My experience is that highly successful managers have a different way of thinking than average managers—which accounts for their strong success. I often have found that the way of thinking employed by subpar or even average managers actually undermines or sabotages their performance. The following nine ways of thinking are essential to the success of any top-performing manager.

## Number 1: It's Not about Me

In the first chapter of this book, "Why Managers Struggle," we discussed managers who get caught up in their own self-importance. I offered the example of how some managers become victims of what I like to call the "all-about-me syndrome." Further, I showed how these managers often get hung up on their own self-importance.

Let's face it: being a manager can be a heady position. As a manager, you can tell people what to do because you are the boss. You may get to fly to far-off places, ride in limousines, and stay in nice hotels, or get invited to present a speech, talk with news reporters, and maybe even appear on television. Given all these benefits of your position, it would be easy to become absorbed with yourself. On any given day, you might think it really is "all about me."

But I'm afraid that is not the mindset of a top performer.

When I became president of Ameritech's cellular subsidiary, Ameritech Mobile, the chairman of Ameritech told me something that has stayed with me ever since. He said I would be managing an entire company, and as the company's most senior manager, I should always remember that the "stripes" I have been given are on the coat I wear, not on the person who wears the coat. He cautioned me to not let the job go to my head because when I take the coat off, I will just be a person like any other. Further, he said I should respect the position I had been given and use it only in ways to benefit our shareholders, customers, and employees.

Those words gave me a lot to think about. I decided no matter what my job, I would never make it about me; rather, my role as a manager would always be about the company, the organization, and its people. I thought of this as the "stripes rule" and reminded myself of it often over the years.

During my career, I came to easily recognize managers who didn't understand the stripes rule. For example, when managers use the words "I" and "my" rather than "we" and "our" when describing the organization they manage or when talking about results, it's a dead giveaway that their mindset is a bit self-centered.

Another sign that managers may be violating the stripes rule is when you start repeatedly seeing their names and faces in newspapers and industry publications, on the covers of magazines, or even on television commercials. Managers who begin to enjoy such self-promotion should recall seventeenth-century historian Thomas Fuller's words, "Fools' names, like fools' faces, are often seen in public places."

> **Successful managers don't get trapped into thinking it's all about them.**

Successful managers don't get trapped into thinking it's all about them. Instead, they know that a company, or an organization within a company, is not made of any one person: it is the sum of all its resources and people.

## Number 2: It's Important to Keep Your Cool

The most successful managers I've worked with over the years have been demanding bosses, but they've also always been respectful. Sure, from time to time they'd been upset when, for example, a goal was missed or an assignment wasn't completed on time, but even then, they always kept their cool. They didn't yell, scream, or pound their fists on their desks. They didn't call their employees "stupid" or talk poorly of them behind their backs. Rather, they dealt with the situation at hand in a calm, unemotional manner. They were polite, but firm, and worked to find a resolution to the issues rather than to place blame. They sought assurances that the situation would not happen again. Nonetheless, the employees always knew they had let their manager down and their manager was disappointed.

We noted one of the reasons managers struggle is because they often have their heads in the sand, since they only want to hear good news. Employees then become conditioned not to deliver bad news, worrying that their boss may tend to overreact to it. I believe employees work even harder for managers who keep their cool at all times. Level-headed managers can always be assured that their employees will share information with them, even if it's bad news, and get started on solving the problem rather than allowing it to be ignored.

## Number 3: Know Your People and Know Their Jobs

Good managers know their people: they understand their strengths and their weaknesses and know the parameters of the jobs their employees were hired to do. By this I mean they aren't just familiar with their employees' job descriptions, but they fully comprehend the details of how they do their jobs. Furthermore, good managers can demonstrate how to do the jobs of the people they lead, filling in for them if

> 66 **Good managers know their people: they understand their strengths and their weaknesses and know the parameters of the jobs their employees were hired to do.** 99

necessary. Because they know their people and their jobs, they are able to put their best people where they can have the biggest impact on getting results. I'm sure all this sounds obvious, but I've known quite a few managers who couldn't seem to get it right.

Make sure you have placed people in jobs that meet their skill set and then give them a fair chance to succeed. I often saw what I call the "round-peg-in-a-square-hole syndrome." An individual may have been placed in a position for which he or she didn't have the requisite skills to do the job. The result was predictable: a month later, we would be deciding to terminate the individual without finding out whether he or she was better qualified for another position in the organization.

Here is a real-life example of the round-peg-in-a-square-hole syndrome.

Mark Monteyne was hired as a customer service representative at Bell Atlantic Mobile in 1990. He was fresh out of college with a bachelor's degree in physical education. During the interview process, he demonstrated his very personable and jovial manner and his strong desire to succeed. The job of a customer service rep primarily entails speaking with customers to answer their questions and address any issues or resolve any problems they may be experiencing. It seemed he would be a natural fit at dealing with customers and was hired for the position.

Unfortunately, after a couple months' time, it became clear that Mark was unable to master talking to customers, and understanding and solving their problems, while typing on the computer at the same time. His manager decided Mark couldn't cut it as a service representative and notified human resources that Mark was about to be fired.

During his exit interview, Mark expressed a strong desire to stay with the company and proposed the idea of setting up a fitness center, a task that was more in line with his educational background. He discussed the employee health advantages, potential cost savings, and productivity improvements that his initiative could create. He was incredibly convincing, even passionate, about the advantages to the company.

The result?

He was given the job of setting up and managing the company's first fitness center. Mark, who is now known throughout the company as Coach Mark, is still managing the company's 35 fitness centers, which have now expanded into a companywide health and wellness program. What he told us about cost savings and enhanced productivity was true, but equally important is what fitness centers have done to boost employee morale.

All too often, when employees are not performing in their jobs, managers immediately move to terminate them rather than present a different opportunity or train them for something more suited to their skill set. Clearly, there are instances when it is necessary to sever ties with an employee who has no potential for contributing toward the success of an organization, but there are also times when employees can be given different opportunities in which they can excel. Such was the case with Coach Mark.

## Number 4: Bring Out the Best in Your People

As we have previously discussed, managing is about getting results through your employees' growth, development, and, ultimately, success. As managers, we plan what our people do, we direct their efforts, we inspect what they do, we coach them when necessary, and, when appropriate, we take corrective actions. But what do managers do to make the best efforts of their people even better?

Many employees approach their jobs with the belief that they can only do so much. They may think their abilities are limited or they need to "pace" themselves and therefore strive to do nothing more than what it takes to reach the goals set by their managers. Some lack confidence; others may lack desire. There are still others who simply may not know just how good they can be.

Our challenge as managers is to bring out the very best in our people, even if that means helping them to be better than they really want

> " Our challenge as managers is to bring out the very best in our people, even if that means helping them to be better than they really want to be. "

to be. But here's one caveat: it is not the role of managers to build self-confidence or self-esteem in their people. Building self-esteem is the responsibility of each individual employee.

This statement may sound contrary to so much that has been written in our current culture on the importance of building self-esteem, but I firmly believe the best way to increase self-esteem is for the person to accomplish something he or she thought couldn't be accomplished. Self-esteem is an outgrowth of knowledge and experience—primarily experience.

The role of managers in building self-esteem in their employees is to demonstrate they believe their employees can do more than they think they can. Then managers need to help promote that belief in their employees. Good managers believe in the individuals who work for them and have faith in the personal responsibility of those individuals to rise to the challenge of being the best at what they do.

So what do managers do to bring out the best in their people?

First, don't create artificial situations. Don't send them off to seminars or training programs designed to "build self-confidence." Additionally, motivating speeches, "inspirational" quotations posted in their workplaces, and recognition do almost nothing to develop employees' long-term self-confidence. Similarly, thinking, planning, and brainstorming do little to build lasting self-confidence.

Instead, give employees real work opportunities to enhance their own self-esteem. Coach them to believe in themselves, and place them in situations that are outside of their comfort zone, forcing them to stretch and test their abilities. Before doing so, acknowledge that you recognize you are asking them to complete an assignment they may not be totally comfortable doing. This acknowledgment is a powerful expression of your faith in their capabilities, and the assignment itself represents an action that speaks louder than any words. Further, let them know that if they make a mistake, you will be there to help them. Finally, tell them they will benefit from the experience. After all, your faith in their ability to rise to the occasion is grounded in the sincere belief that their success is reflective of your effort to provide them with an opportunity to grow.

A simple principle may help explain the importance of experience in helping employees grow: *self-confidence begins with taking action.*

Here's an example.

Let's say an employee wants to improve his presentation skills, since public speaking causes him great fear and stress. The manager may give the employee a pep talk to bolster his confidence, or the employee may read a book on making presentations and even talk to others who are skilled at public speaking. In addition, the employee may spend numerous hours planning and preparing a presentation.

Nothing will have a bigger positive impact on such employees' self-confidence, however, than taking the uncomfortable action of consistently getting in front of audiences and making presentations. So the manager in this situation could help build the self-confidence of the employee by scheduling several presentations for him. This is not to say that the manager believes in a sink-or-swim philosophy—i.e., schedule the presentations and see whether the employee succeeds or fails. Good managers would never think of sending their employees out on admittedly difficult tasks without any support. Rather, the good manager might coach the employee during the process and attempt to reinforce the strengths of the employee's presentation while helping to identify any weaknesses and trying to eliminate them.

The key to getting the employee to build his self-confidence in this case is forcing him into an uncomfortable action—getting in front of people to present information to them—even when the thought of doing so is unpleasant for him to consider.

Another method I used to bring out the best in people was simply to ask them to do more. For example, when they told me they were finished with an assignment or had achieved a goal, I would thank them for what they had done so far, compliment them on their good work, and then say something like, "I think you can make this even better." Senior managers who worked directly for me often heard me say, "Great job, but you're not done yet." Invariably, they accepted my challenge and made what they did even better!

Let's say you have a team of sales managers who have achieved their monthly sales goal on the twentieth day of the month. At this point, they may feel they are done for the month because they reached a difficult goal with time to spare. They instinctively set their sights on next month's goal instead of working to get additional sales in the present month. They put plans in motion to move sales that are possible in this month to the next, so that hitting their goals then will be easier. The danger in doing this, of course, is that customers who are ready to buy this month may "cool off" and no longer be willing to do so come next month.

So if sales managers would hit their goals on the twentieth, I would make it a point to see them, congratulate them, and simply say, "You're not done yet," to let them know I expected more sales before the end of the month. I knew that the moment they hit their monthly target, they were in their comfort zone. When I would say, "You're not done yet," they suddenly were forced out of this zone until they made more sales.

## Number 5: Make Yourself a Little Better Every Day

This phrase is a reminder to do better continually by building your management knowledge and skills every single day. Conditions around you—economies, markets, customers, products, organizations—are perpetually changing. Unless you are building your skills continually, your past skills may not be appropriate for these fluctuating conditions, and instead of improving your ability to reach goals and succeed, you will find your performance slipping.

I often wonder when people tell me that they have five years of experience whether they actually do, or if they only have one year of experience repeated five times. If it's the latter, they are performing today with the same skill set they had five years ago.

I don't think managers necessarily get better by virtue only of their experience. They also don't get better by just reading a management book like this one or by attending a seminar, although some think they do.

In both these cases, they frequently fail to get better if they don't translate concepts, ideas, and skills into management strengths. The key is the ability to take a concept, an idea, or a skill and turn it into daily behavior through commitment and practice.

So being exposed to management ideas, concepts, and skills is not what makes managers better. Managers will only get better when they take responsibility for getting better. It is important for managers to systematically improve their skill set by taking responsibility, demonstrating commitment, and practicing their skills.

Personally, I have always had a goal of learning at least one new thing every day. Recently, I've been learning about writing books. Sure, on some days I might learn more than just one thing, but the goal is at least one per day. This attitude toward learning makes a difference in the growth of a manager.

## Number 6: "Telling It Like It Is" Leads to Improvement

Many of us have worked at one time or another for managers who had trouble having a direct conversation—one in which they actually said what they really meant. Instead, they would use "weasel words" for what they were trying to say, being indirect and circuitous and not really getting to the point. Often, managers were leaving employees guessing about what was really meant.

Many times, this is the case when it's time to deliver bad news. I'll be one of the first to admit that discussing bad news, whether with a group of people or an individual, is one of the most difficult things managers have to do and is precisely why a lot of managers are not good at it—some can't bring themselves to do it at all.

However, uncomfortable conversations can create positive changes when people clearly understand improvements are required. I have always believed communicating directly—whether it was explaining poor results to an entire company or simply letting someone know

I was not satisfied with his or her performance—was essential to improvement.

Good managers will tell it like it is, regardless if the news is good or bad. They know it's best to speak honestly and openly at all times. If there is bad news to deliver, get it out and get it over with. Say it clearly and concisely, don't try to sugarcoat it, and say it with respect. The people you work for and the people who work for you deserve to hear the facts and see the data. Without this information, it's difficult for your employees to make the positive changes necessary for improvement.

### Number 7: Don't Throw Your People under the Bus, but Know When to Let Them Off

A few managers I've encountered over the years have had a tendency to give up too soon on people who worked for them. These were the same managers who blamed their employees when things didn't go precisely as planned.

I have always believed that, as the boss, when something wasn't going quite right, I was the one responsible for fixing it, and if there was blame to be placed, I accepted it. What I refused to do was blame someone who worked for me for any failure on the part of the organization I managed.

As manager, I was also responsible for identifying the strengths and the weaknesses of the people who worked for me. When I saw weaknesses in an individual, I told the individual privately what I had observed and my expectations for improvement. In my experience, very rarely did I find anyone who didn't

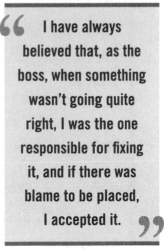

I have always believed that, as the boss, when something wasn't going quite right, I was the one responsible for fixing it, and if there was blame to be placed, I accepted it.

improve once a weakness was clearly brought to the person's attention. Incidentally, this is probably obvious, but I feel compelled to state it: managers shouldn't have just one approach for everybody when working to correct a weakness, and it should be recognized that not everyone is motivated in the same way. A number of distinct approaches may be necessary in improving the same deficiencies in different people.

From time to time, unfortunately, there were those employees who didn't improve. In such instances, it was my job to know when to "let them off the bus." One of the most difficult things for a manager to do is fire someone, but there are times when it is exactly what needs to be done for the good of the entire organization.

Firing decisions, however, are often made prematurely. I think it is essential to take the time necessary and provide the coaching required to help an individual improve. My advice would always be to not give up on an individual too soon—not only because it's the right thing to do but because you've already made an investment in the person. You cannot afford to lose that investment.

As a manager, you also need to recognize when you've done all you can do. If you reach that point and the employee is still failing, the best action for the individual and for the entire organization is to separate right away. A mistake managers too often make is prolonging (or avoiding) the inevitable. When this foot-dragging happens, others who work for the manager begin to question the manager's ability to make the right decision.

## Number 8: It Takes Courage

There are times when it takes courage to tell it like it is. Perhaps it's necessary to deliver bad news to your boss, or tell your boss that you disagree with him or her, or explain that you believe something you were told to do is wrong. There are occasions where it may be necessary to voice your conflicting point of view: good managers don't hesitate to speak up when they disagree.

Managers may also need to make decisions or do things that not only are difficult but may open them up to criticism. What follows is a personal example of just such an instance.

In 2004, the wireless industry in the United States was making plans to publish a directory that would list the names and telephone numbers of everyone who subscribed to cell phone service. The wireless carriers saw it as a means to increase their revenue streams because they believed that by listing everyone's cell phone telephone number in a phone book, people would make more calls. I believed most Verizon Wireless customers would not be happy about receiving more calls on their cell phones, particularly if they received unwanted ones, such as some of the annoying tape-recorded sales and telemarketing calls they already had to deal with on their landlines.

Several CEOs of other wireless companies were strongly in favor of moving ahead with the directory and were angry with me when I opposed the effort. I began receiving letters and phone calls accusing me of being an obstructionist. Several meetings were held to try to convince me of the "irrationality" of my position. Regardless of the mounting pressure to get me to change my mind, in a speech before a large audience of industry analysts and consultants, I said, "As an industry, let's stop pushing something on customers that they clearly don't want. It's a dumb idea." Further, I said Verizon Wireless would not participate in a telephone directory, and our decision was final.

I certainly didn't win any friends within the wireless industry, but I did receive many letters from Verizon customers applauding the decision. I'm convinced that as difficult as it was to buck the rest of the industry and forgo what would probably have been more revenue for our company, I made the right call. And in the long run, I think more people signed up for Verizon service because they viewed us as a company willing to do the right things for our customers.

### Number 9: Never Set the Tone for Whining and Complaining

Much has already been said about the importance of casting a positive shadow, so I won't repeat it here other than to say the best managers I've worked with are perpetually optimistic. Of course, they don't whine about anything, but in addition they don't complain. When managers tolerate whining and complaining, from either themselves or their employees, they set the tone for commiseration, which is always a huge waste of time and energy. I have always believed there is no room for self-pity in any organization I have managed.

## YOUR MINDSET

These nine ways of thinking constitute the mindset of a successful manager. Each will go a long way toward helping you achieve your results. Remember, actions speak louder than words, and managers who insist their employees continually grow by challenging them to improve themselves allow them to demonstrate their success through their actions and achievement. Self-esteem can only grow from within an individual, but a manager's mindset can ensure that opportunities for employees to enhance their self-esteem will be abundant and encouraged.

These nine ways of thinking will go a long way toward helping you achieve your results. Having seen how a manager's mindset can be an asset or a liability to his or her performance, we will next explore how a manager copes with distractions as another opportunity for overcoming a major barrier to effective management.

## CHAPTER SUMMARY POINTS

1. Managers' mindsets reflect how they view the world, their job, and the people around them.
2. While a mindset can be changed, the best managers often have developed a positive mindset instinctively.
3. Managers can help cultivate a positive mindset in their employees by demonstrating and maintaining their own positive mindset.
4. While self-esteem can only be enhanced by an individual, good managers can seek and promote enhancement opportunities for their employees.

## CHAPTER ACTION GUIDE

Managers, here's a suggestion: take the nine recommendations for building a positive mindset discussed in this chapter and write them down on a sheet of paper. Keep that list handy and refer to it occasionally. How closely does your performance that day, that week, or that year meet the objectives of these nine items? By treating them as guideposts along the path toward a positive mindset, you will be able to chart your progress by frequently evaluating where you stand in relation to them.

Chapter 8

# MANAGING DISTRACTIONS

The more managers focus on distractions, the less they focus on results. And in today's world, e-mails present a distraction. Certainly, when people are asked what they do for a living, no one says, "I write and answer e-mails." Yet that's what a lot of people spend their time doing. According to an article by K. J. McCorry, published in August 2009, more than 50 *billion* e-mails were sent every day in 2001.[1] Five years later, it was up to 6 *trillion* messages. Last year, that worked out to 160 messages per day per office worker. At least 88 percent of it is junk—spam, commercial newsletters, or other unsolicited messages.

Answering e-mails isn't getting work done. One of the most time-wasting e-mails I've gotten recently is from a company offering a seminar in "how to sort through e-mails, texts, and voice messages." I had to wonder whether their instruction would include how to deal with future e-mails from their own company.

E-mails are just one of the many distractions a manager faces. In the rest of this chapter, we'll discuss this and other diversions that keep you from doing your job if you let them distract you.

## E-MAIL AS A DISTRACTION

When I was at Verizon Wireless, our vice president of corporate communications, Jim Gerace, issued guidelines on the proper use of e-mail. I found his guidance very valuable (and yes, he did issue these guidelines via e-mail):

- ▶ E-mail should bring closure to work, not create more work.
- ▶ Before you write an e-mail, ask yourself if calling or visiting the recipient will bring better communication.
- ▶ Keep e-mails short. Pretend that the recipient isn't going to open the e-mail and you need to make your point in just the subject line or the space in the preview pane.
- ▶ Don't assume other people are staring at their screens, waiting for your e-mail.
- ▶ If just one person needs information or clarification, don't send it to a group.
- ▶ Never send an e-mail when you're angry. If you must write one in such a state, wait until the next day and read it over to decide whether you really want to send it.
- ▶ Be careful what you put in writing. Pretend anything you write will be subpoenaed, read before Congress, or leaked to the press.
- ▶ Stay accountable. Sending an e-mail doesn't transfer responsibility.
- ▶ E-mail is never an acceptable excuse for not getting something done. If you need a reply to an e-mail before you can do your job, get the information another way. Don't send another e-mail

asking why you didn't get an answer to the first one; call or visit the person you need information from.

▶ Before answering, or even reading, an e-mail, ask yourself, "What is the worst that can happen if I delete this?"

▶ Don't spend more than five minutes dealing with an e-mail. When you go over this limit, stop and make a phone call.

▶ If your computer makes an audible signal that you've received an e-mail, turn the sound off. I'd suggest you do the same on your cell phone.

▶ Don't judge how much you've accomplished by how many e-mails you've sent.

▶ If you don't think you can go to a meeting without peeking at your e-mail, don't attend the meeting.

Jim's advice on whether or when to even use e-mail is almost as important as his warning to always be careful what you write in an e-mail. When I worked at Bell Atlantic Mobile, one of our managers was asked to complete a report that would get us ranked by an outside analyst. This manager found the questions difficult and felt the outside analyst's firm was going to rate us low, no matter what he wrote in his report. So he forwarded the analyst's request to 20 executives at Bell Atlantic, adding his comment that he was sure the analyst would give us a bad report and that the analyst "was a dope." The problem was that after he added the 20 names of Bell Atlantic executives, he hit "reply" instead of "forward" to his e-mail. You can imagine what happened: the analyst got the e-mail. Sure enough, we received a bad rating from his firm that year.

Don't get me wrong: e-mail is a wonderful thing. As suggested in our earlier chapter on results, your goal to check e-mail three times a day—morning, noon, and late afternoon—should be sufficient for most managers. Just don't keep checking it continually during the entire day. Reading and answering e-mail is important, but it's not your job. Don't be constantly attached to your e-mail. Remember the Four Fundamentals: your job is growing revenue, getting new customers, keeping your current customers, and eliminating costs.

## INTERNET DISTORTIONS

If you went to business school in the 1960s, '70s, or '80s, you didn't have any courses on electronic communication because very few people had access to the Internet back then. But to be a manager today, you need to deal with the fact that information of all kinds is instantly available through all types of electronic devices.

The first action many people take now when they want to know about a company or an individual is to consult the Internet, probably Googling the organization's or person's name. Of course, that doesn't mean that information on the Internet is accurate or unbiased.

On Labor Day 2009, Massey Energy held a "Friends of America" rally in West Virginia to support the coal mining industry. Conservative talk show host Sean Hannity was a featured speaker. A local Verizon Wireless manager decided this would be a good opportunity to recruit customers, and he rented a booth.

Liberal bloggers learned about the arrangement and posted it on the Internet. While harmless enough—a telecommunications company trying to sell phones and cell phone subscriptions—the story soon took on a life of its own. Bloggers posited that supporting coal mining was antienvironment. Headlines appeared with statements such as "Verizon Wireless Joins Massey Energy to Celebrate Mountaintop Removal and Climate Change Denial" and "Verizon Wireless: Open

Mouth, Insert Mountain." Readers were given my e-mail address and told to send me protests. In defending our action, one of our top people joked that a critic "lived in a tree for a while"—a statement that, of course, ended up posted on the Internet.

Although the connection between renting a sales booth and supporting the despoliation of the earth seems far-fetched, it gained momentum because of the breadth and reach of the Internet and people's tendency to believe negative information. Other blogs attacked Verizon as being against clean air, and letters came into headquarters criticizing the company for being unfriendly to the environment. Our Verizon public relations team fought back with statements and editorials, but it took a long time for the perception that we "hated the environment" to go away. And all this occurred because of one innocuous sales and marketing act by a local employee that was picked up and singled out by an initially small number of bloggers. The lesson to be learned from this is simple: don't be personally distracted by a lot of electronic noise, always place your message in the right hands, and be careful what you put in writing.

> " **Don't be personally distracted by a lot of electronic noise, always place your message in the right hands, and be careful what you put in writing.** "

These days, you can even be the victim of a cyberattack for something your competitors did! After the 9/11 events, Dr Pepper put a new design on its soda cans showing the Statue of Liberty with the caption, "One Nation . . . Indivisible." A few people took offense because they felt the caption appeared to be a rewriting of the Pledge of Allegiance, which includes the phrase, "One nation under God, indivisible . . ." They alleged Dr Pepper was being atheistic or unpatriotic in not including the entire phrase. In the three months that Dr Pepper produced and distributed the

18 million cans with this design, it got about 200 complaints. It explained its position on its Web site, and its bottom line wasn't affected.

But a few years later, Dr Pepper's rivals began getting complaints. E-mails began circulating that Coke and Pepsi had "taken 'under God' out of the Pledge." The two companies could only explain that they did not produce Dr Pepper and had never put the phrase "One Nation . . . Indivisible" on any of their products.

Never underestimate the power of e-mail chains, Web sites, and blogs to distribute information—regardless of its accuracy!

## The Man Who Turned Down the iPhone

False rumors may affect you as an individual, as well as your organization. There are even Web sites dedicated to spreading negative stories about people, regardless of the truth. You might find your neighbors called the "most obnoxious family alive," bad drivers, or incapable of being faithful. Not only do these sources post slanderous comments about you anonymously, but some will even post a Google map of where you live. Considering tracking down the gossip who slandered you and suing the culprit? Think again: these Web sites have already taken this into account, and they include references to software that enables posters to hide their Internet addresses.

While the Internet has made communication faster and easier than ever before, it has also made the spread of misinformation equally instantaneous and far-reaching.

For example, if you haven't already Googled me, here's something you might find: "Denny Strigl is the guy who turned down the iPhone." Yes, my reputation in certain venues is the CEO who could have partnered with one of the most talked-about products of the decade but instead turned it down. This makes for an interesting case study on how people and organizations acquire Internet reputations—and how they must deal with managing them.

Here are the facts: In 2005, Steve Jobs of Apple visited Verizon with an idea for a new kind of phone. I'll have to say we were interested in the product he described, but we weren't the only company Jobs approached. He went to AT&T and others with the same idea.

As our discussions with Apple evolved, it became clear that Apple was more interested in partnering with AT&T. At the time the technology AT&T deployed, called GSM, was used in more countries around the world, whereas Verizon's technology, CDMA, was limited primarily to the United States and a few other countries. In other words, if Apple made a GSM iPhone, there was opportunity to sell many more phones worldwide. So a partnership between AT&T and Apple simply made better economic sense for Apple.

To make a long story short, back in 2005 Verizon never really had an opportunity to strike a deal with Apple about the iPhone because Apple's choice was to produce a GSM phone. Instead, Steve Jobs and my counterpart at AT&T, Stan Sigmund, reached a deal, and AT&T became the first wireless carrier to offer the iPhone. Of course, it turned out to be a good result for both Apple and AT&T.

But if people wanted to think of me as the "iPhone Refuser," I was okay with that. I didn't let it affect me; I maintained my focus and kept on getting results.

So those are the facts—even though I'm still the "guy who turned down the iPhone."

(*Note:* CDMA technology is now capable of operating around the world. An Apple-Verizon iPhone became available in February 2011.)

What is the lesson from this incident?

Keep your head down, keep focused on results, and ignore rumors unless they impact your Four Fundamentals (grow revenue, get new customers, keep the customers you have, and eliminate costs). Just be aware that the higher your profile, the bigger a target you become for people who may have some other agenda.

Attacks that start elsewhere can also be escalated by the Internet. Several years ago, the Communications Workers of America (CWA) union decided I was the one responsible for thwarting its attempts to organize Verizon Wireless. Not only did the union put my picture on its Web site, but it got personal, even picketing my home. At the time, I was on the board of trustees of Canisius College, a Roman Catholic institution in Buffalo, New York. CWA picketed a trustees meeting I attended, claiming that my "antiunion" stance violated the Vatican's policy on the right of workers to organize. The college newspaper joined the bandwagon.

My reaction was simple: although the situation was personally upsetting, I did not allow these attacks to distract me; I kept doing what I was doing, maintaining my belief that a union was not in the best interest of our workers—and I certainly didn't cave in to CWA's demands. And the Canisius trustees elected me chairman of the board at their next meeting.


## How to Respond to Attacks

Often the best response to lies in the age of instant information is to ignore them. Keep your focus on your business, and your success will usually make people forget the rumors, slander, or false accusations against you. Every organization has a watercooler or coffee machine where people gather and exchange gossip—trading statements like, "I hear there are going to be layoffs," or "Did you hear the boss is on his way out?" You know not to respond to everything you hear, and you should treat most gossip arising from the Internet the same way.

Fighting back on the Internet may be a waste of time. One company found false information in a chat room posted by someone who claimed to be its CEO. It decided it would be fruitless to have the real CEO go online and refute the false information because readers wouldn't know who was telling the truth.

> ❝ **Keep your focus on your business, and your success will usually make people forget the rumors, slander, or false accusations against you.** ❞

Is it worth suing to protect your individual reputation? Suing is hard when comments are posted anonymously. You can sue anonymous "John Does" or subpoena Internet service providers to learn who posted the remarks, but it's a long, expensive, and difficult process.

Even when you know who wrote the lies, it's hard to win a case against the person. Sidney Blumenthal learned this firsthand when Matt Drudge posted a defamatory report on his Web site about Blumenthal. The Drudge Report is a conservative blog, and Blumenthal worked for the Clinton White House at the time. Drudge wrote that court records existed proving Blumenthal had committed violence against his wife.

There was nothing to substantiate the report, and Drudge retracted it the next day. But Blumenthal sued Drudge and America Online (AOL), which carried his column. The court ruled that AOL was not liable for false information it carried, and Blumenthal eventually settled out of court—paying Drudge $2,500 for "travel expenses."

## DEALING WITH PERSONAL ATTACKS

When I became general sales manager with Wisconsin Telephone, we had the worst sales results in the Bell System. I was assigned to get the organization into shape.

I've mentioned elsewhere what I did to turn Wisconsin Telephone around. Among other things, I made it clear it was no longer acceptable to lose a customer. Any salesperson who did so had to go before the company's Lost Customer Review Board and describe why the customer was lost, then present a plan to win the customer back.

This was a tough-minded process. Frankly, it was not designed to be a pleasant experience. Rather, it was meant to stress the importance of doing everything reasonably and ethically possible to avoid losing customers. When members of the review board determined someone messed up, harsh action was taken—up to and including time off without pay and even firing. The review board helped change the behavior of the sales force, and results turned around quickly.

The reason I'm recounting this is not to tell you what a wonderful manager I was; it's to describe my personal feelings during the turnaround period. Frankly, it was hell to go through. A lot of people didn't like what I was doing, and they made their feelings known, though usually not to my face. Sometimes the gossip reached me, as when someone told me, "I heard someone say you're a real S.O.B." My response always was, "Thank you for the information." There was no use reacting to the criticism; I couldn't win that battle. I let my results—which spoke louder and clearer than anything I could have said to my detractors—answer the critics.

The more you respond to criticism, the more credence you give it. Keep your head down, plow ahead, and remain focused on results. If negative stories are circulating about you, the results you produce will show people that your detractors were just demonstrating sour grapes all along. The power of your character will come through in the long run.

> ❝ The more you respond to criticism, the more credence you give it. Keep your head down, plow ahead, and remain focused on results. ❞

## OTHER DISTRACTIONS

With all its benefits, the Internet has brought more distractions than just the lightning-fast spread of rumors. Instant communication can also mean instant distractions.

For example, whenever you go to a public performance today, the sponsor always reminds the audience to turn off all cell phones, pagers, and other electronic devices. And if it's a performance with an intermission, you're asked to remember to turn your phone off again after you use it during the break. This sort of warning shouldn't be necessary, but it seems a fact of modern life.

Equally annoying are people who text-message during meetings. When attending operations reviews, I had a simple solution: although we were in the cell phone business, at the beginning of the meeting I announced that as a courtesy to the managers making presentations, it would be appreciated if the attendees would put their electronic devices out of sight. Further, those who texted or checked their e-mail during the meeting would be fined a $10 penalty. If it happened a second time, the penalty would be increased to $10,000. Everyone got the message, by the way, and no one ever had to pay.

Why do people text during meetings? Most offenders would say it's a way to multitask and use time efficiently. But research shows that dividing attention between competing tasks instead of handling them one at a time is far less efficient. And most people who do it admit that it's rude to text while someone else is talking.

If you're holding a meeting, insist attendees put their devices in pockets, purses, or briefcases. And if the meeting runs long (I always advise holding short ones), call a break so colleagues can check their messages.

## BE IN CHARGE OF YOUR OWN DAY

It's important to take charge of your own day. Don't let someone else be in control. You will have distractions coming at you from all different directions. You will have a constant flow of e-mails, text messages, phone calls, and phone messages that can interrupt your day. It's a constant barrage.

As we discussed in Chapter 3, our chapter on a manager's obligation to focus on results, it takes discipline to be in control of your own workday. Each distraction we've looked at usually places an immediate demand on you, gaining your attention, and sometimes there is an immediate emotional response to it. This will happen minute by minute if you let it. There is almost an urgency placed on each distraction, *whether it's important or not*. Remember, not all urgent distractions are important in relationship to your goals; in fact, I would say most are not. Sometimes, when you check on each distraction the moment it occurs, it simply becomes a poor time-consuming habit.

> "Sometimes, when you check on each distraction the moment it occurs, it simply becomes a poor time-consuming habit."

It takes a disciplined mindset to focus on the Four Fundamentals and leave distractions for certain times of the day. If, in fact, there is an immediate, important matter from your manager or a customer that truly *is* urgent, I'm sure the person will know how to get to you quickly.

Many of these urgent distractions have nothing to do with what is important to you and your company in driving results. So if you are going to be successful, it's essential to manage your day by limiting the distractions that can otherwise control it—and you. In our next chapter, the final chapter of this book, you will see how the message of each of the preceding chapters contributes toward the creation of a culture of success.

## Chapter Summary Points

1. Reading and answering e-mail can distract you from doing your job. Don't let it consume you.
2. Don't let Internet "distortions" distract you. Stay focused on the Four Fundamentals.
3. Let your results answer your personal critics. As a general rule, reacting to criticism begets more criticism.
4. Be in charge of your own day. Avoid letting someone or something else control your day.

## Chapter Action Guide

1. Conduct this test for yourself. For several days, review e-mails and text messages first thing in the morning, at noon, and late in the day before you go home. Examine the results and see if you are spending more time on the Four Fundamentals. Then make it a new habit for yourself.
2. During the course of your day, stay focused on the important activities that drive results in the Four Fundamentals. Important activities are those that significantly contribute to results.

## Chapter 9

# Building a
# Culture of
# Performance

In early January every year, Verizon Wireless held meetings at work locations throughout the country to introduce the goals for the new year, to discuss new market strategies and programs, and to generally get employees refocused on the Four Fundamentals. These "kickoff" meetings, as we called them, were also an opportunity to celebrate successes from the prior year and candidly discuss how we could improve the business going forward.

In January 2004, after merging several companies into one, Verizon Wireless had gotten past the integration activities required to assemble the largest wireless communications provider in the United States. The new company was operating well, but I was unsatisfied with the speed at which we were realizing merger synergies and capitalizing on our new market strength. I remember thinking that we were leaving a lot on the table and not reaching our potential quick enough. Something was missing.

As we were pulling together the material for the first kickoff meeting, my communications team handed me a one-page document that the team said would help bring together everything we were asking our employees to do. It was not a summary of our goals for the coming year; rather, it was the anthology of our core beliefs, values, and aspirations. This one piece of paper managed to capture everything I had been trying to instill in our employees. It was the way we had been conducting business in Verizon Wireless's predecessor companies for the previous 13 years, and it showed how we wanted to continue doing business in the future. It was exactly what we needed to get everyone on the same page.

At the end of each kickoff meeting that year, I delivered a speech to employees using the words from that one page. The words became our company credo and the synopsis of our company culture.

I didn't assemble a task force to write our company credo, I didn't hire a consultant, nor did I assemble a focus group to test out what concepts would fly. The credo reflected my core beliefs and spoke about the actions I had taken as CEO that set the tone for our company culture, and it was in action long before it was committed to paper.

I consider company culture the underlying character of an organization—its lifeblood. It's the attitude that employees display and the actions that employees take. As we've said before, the attitude, or "shadow," of the leader sets the tone for the whole organization.

> **Culture drives an organization every day: it's not only what you do, but also how you do it.**

Culture is the values everyone in the company shares—whether it's sales volume, profits, output, or numbers served that you consider most important—as the company strives to attain its results. Culture drives an organization every day: it's not only what you do, but also how you do it.

Long before the Verizon Wireless credo came to be, I scratched out a note on a blue-lined sheet of paper and labeled it, "What Is Important." You can see it here.

**"What Is Important," thoughts that I began to set down in 1984 and that helped me stay focused throughout the years**

*continued*

2.

8. work Habits (con't)
   - Be punctual - start meeting on time,
     end on time,
       accomplish things
   - Expect opposing points of view -
     Solicit them - but when
     a decision is made - move
     together.
   - Eliminate unnecessary activity
   - Compliment for a job well done
   - Never allow whining, excuses,
       finger pointing or commiseration.

→ 9. Loyalty - To the Corporation
             To the task to be performed
   - to one another

→ 10. Creativity and Innovation: In everything — make
       things better, try new things, be
       open to ideas. Customer focus

11. Customer Service must Improve Immediately

   Shallow
     of leaders
   - reduce bureaucracy
     empower people
       constant attention
       to driving down costs.

I wrote the note in 1984, the same year the federal courts broke up the company I was working for, AT&T, and ushered in a new era of communications. It was a time of change and uncertainty for those of us working in the telecommunications industry, but that piece of paper helped me stay focused on what was really important. I kept it in my top desk drawer, reviewed it often, and updated it periodically. Every time I moved on to a different job, I read my note to the people who worked for me to let them know what I thought was important and how they could expect me to operate. The note evolved into a statement of the values I believed in.

Here are the concepts I wrote on that old piece of paper over the years that might be a starting point for any organization's culture:

1. Customers:
   ▶ Customer service is key.
   ▶ Our job is to create products customers value.
   ▶ Quality and reliability are key to keeping our customers and getting more.
   ▶ Our focus is always outside our business and on our customers, never inside the business or on ourselves.
2. Results:
   ▶ We make things happen; we get things done.
   ▶ Everyone is accountable.
   ▶ We aim to do things right the first time.
   ▶ Our best is made better every day.
   ▶ When we say we will do something, we do it.
3. People:
   ▶ We are fair and consistent.
   ▶ We respect and trust one another.
   ▶ Teamwork enables us to serve our customers better and faster.
   ▶ Encouraging diversity and personal development is the right way to act and good for business.
3. Communication:
   ▶ We are open, candid, and direct.

▶ We are honest about every single thing we say and do.

▶ We communicate often: with communication, more *is* better.

▶ Everyone has an obligation to constructively dissent, but when a decision is made, we move together.

4. Work habits:

▶ We do the right things in dealing with customers, suppliers, owners, and even competitors.

▶ We eliminate unnecessary activity.

▶ We are punctual in everything we do.

▶ We are always courteous to our customers, of course, but to each other as well.

▶ We all roll up our sleeves to get work done.

▶ We don't tolerate whining, finger-pointing, or commiseration.

▶ Excuses are never acceptable.

When we created Verizon Wireless in 2000, we were combining many separate wireless companies with unique legacies, traditions, and, yes, cultures. To realize our vision of the first great national wireless company, I knew multiple cultures, or companies within the company, would not work. As the CEO, I needed to set the tone for our new organization, so I again referred to that piece of paper I scribbled in 1984. I applied those concepts from day one, and I suggested my leadership team do so as well.

Then, after three years of integration work accomplished by applying these above principles, Jim Gerace, vice president of corporate communications, wrote the Verizon Wireless credo on his own initiative. Jim will tell you it was the easiest piece he ever wrote because he simply recorded the behaviors he observed over the previous years.

Maybe so, but when he handed me the credo before our first kickoff meeting in 2004, I knew that it captured exactly the values we had been working for years to build and that I wanted in the company. Here's the Verizon Wireless credo:

## Verizon Wireless credo

### We Are Verizon Wireless

We have work because our customers value our high quality wireless communications service. A dropped or incomplete call is not acceptable. Everything we do we build on a strong network foundation. The quality and reliability of the product we deliver is paramount. Customers pay us to provide them with a wireless communications service that they can rely on. We focus outward on the customer, not inward. We make it easy for customers to do business with us, by listening, anticipating and responding to their needs. We know our products and can explain them to customers. We plan less and execute more. We are accountable and we follow through with a sense of urgency. We know that having the highest ethical standards is a competitive advantage. We view having a clean store window as more important than having a corner office. We know teamwork enables us to serve our customers better and faster. We embrace diversity and personal development not only because it's the right thing to do, but also because it's smart business. We are driven not by ego but by accomplishments. We respect and trust one another, communicating openly, candidly and directly since any other way is unfair and a waste of time. We don't need witnesses or paper trails to our conversations. Our word is enough. We voice our opinion and exercise constructive dissent, and then rally around the agreed-upon action with our full support. Any one of us can deliver a view or idea to anyone else, and listen to and value another's view regardless of title or level. Ideas live and die on their merits rather than where they were invented. We believe integrity is at the core of who we are. It establishes the trust that is critical to the relationships we have. We are committed to do the right thing and follow sound business practices in dealing with our customers, suppliers, owners and competitors. Our competitors are not enemies; they are challengers. We are good corporate citizens and share our success with the community to make the world in which we work better than it was yesterday. We know that bigness is not our strength, best is our strength. Bureaucracy is an enemy. We fight every day to stay "small" and keep bureaucracy out. We are more agile than companies a fraction of our size, because we act fast and take risks every day. We see crisis and change as opportunities, not threats. We run to a crisis, not away. Change energizes us. We work hard, take action and get things done. Our actions produce measurable results.

**We work 24x7 because our customers depend on us 24x7.**
We know our best was good for today. Tomorrow we'll do better.
**We are VERIZON WIRELESS.**

*veri**zon**wireless*

> " Simply stating your values and posting them on the wall is not good enough. As managers, we have to model the behavior we want and live it every day. "

A word of caution: simply stating your values and posting them on the wall is not good enough. As managers, we have to model the behavior we want and live it every day. Lowell McAdam, who was president of Verizon Wireless when I retired, likes to describe culture as a muscle that needs to be exercised every day or it will weaken. Lowell is constantly on the lookout for opportunities to strengthen his organization's culture.

On his way into an employee meeting at one of Verizon Wireless's field offices in 2008, Lowell noticed dozens of employees walking away from the room where the meeting was being held. He stopped several employees and asked where they were going, and the response was that the room was full. The employees were visibly disappointed that they wouldn't get to hear what the CEO had to say while many of their colleagues would. Lowell went into the room, came out a back door, and waved in all the "overflow" employees for standing spots in the front of the room. After the meeting, he followed up on the events that led to turning away employees. It turns out that some people assumed that the CEO would want all employees in seats and not standing around the room, possibly distracting the CEO. Lowell saw it another way. He understood the value of communicating to his employees, as many as possible of them, face-to-face, and he also realized the value of demonstrating that commitment to them in real time.

In the rest of this chapter, we'll discuss how you form an organization's culture, how you spread it through your company, and how you get everyone on the team to live up to it.

## What Culture Is Not

If you ask most people on the street what "culture" means to them, they'd probably cite high-minded arts or maybe the ethnic groups they studied in that anthropology class in college (or even Culture Club, Boy George's old band).

Most managers will tell you that culture is the underlying character of an organization—but many still don't understand what it *really* is.

Some think you can build a culture by putting signs or slogans up around the organization, proclaiming how you want things done. That doesn't cut it. Simply stating what your culture is doesn't mean people are going to follow it. Culture must be demonstrated every day: it must be lived.

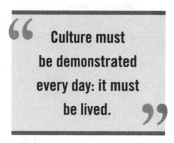

" Culture must be demonstrated every day: it must be lived. "

Still other managers think culture is a feel-good adjunct to the way things really work. To them, it's touchy-feely, one of the nice-to-have add-ons that twenty-first-century organizational thinking demands. I call this the "Kumbaya" approach, with images of everyone sitting around a campfire singing that old Peter, Paul, and Mary folk song. This won't do you much good, and it isn't really culture at all. Besides, research shows that happy employees don't necessarily bring excellent results, but excellent results will make employees happy.

Some cynical managers consider culture just the flavor of the day. They'll tell you it's how the boss (who may be fresh from a seminar on building culture) says we're supposed to operate. Come next week (and a different seminar), the culture may change to keep up with the latest fashion, the cynics will say. Some companies will even feed the cynics by putting someone in charge of culture. Still others will talk about culture but not do anything to cultivate or foster it within a company.

> " **Research shows that happy employees don't necessarily bring excellent results, but excellent results will make employees happy.** "

These are all examples of the "cultural headwinds." As a manager focused on results, you need to overcome this resistance by living, or "exercising," your organization's culture every day—and this means in good times and bad. This is a critical point. You cannot build a sustainable, high-performance culture if it is a culture of convenience. During times of stress and crisis, you can't set principles aside. If you violate your values when you are under pressure, you severely damage your efforts to build a strong culture.

What if you unintentionally do something or say something that contradicts the culture? Shortly after we introduced the Verizon Wireless credo, one of our regional managers was chairing a department head meeting in which some serious issues needed to be addressed. During the heated discussion, she suddenly realized that she violated the value of respect by responding sarcastically toward comments made by a department head. First, she immediately apologized to the group for violating a core value. Then as soon as she returned to her office, she sent an e-mail to the entire region, detailing what had occurred. She apologized and told them that living by the credo has to be top of mind for every employee, herself included. She admitted it may not always come naturally at first. She concluded by asking for a redoubling of efforts on everyone's part to live the culture. This was a symbolic act to drive home the importance of modeling core values.

## How to Build Your Organization's Culture

An organization's culture is determined by how you, as a manager, behave. It can't start from the bottom of the company, nor can it be sustained that way. Even if lower-level employees have established a positive culture, the boss can sabotage it. Remember, culture reflects the "shadow of the leader." It's the values you not only talk about but actually *live*.

Begin by understanding the values you work by and the ones you believe would produce superior and sustainable results if the entire organization shared them. I've described some of the characteristics of Verizon Wireless's culture that are captured in the credo, but let's take it further and explore how I tried to embody these values as a leader, beginning with the five core principles I outlined in 1984.

## Customers

The first thing any company or organization needs is not capital or revenue, but a purpose. A leader must establish early for his or her organization why he or she is asking people to do what they do. For me, I always grounded my teams by focusing them first and foremost on the customer. When we all understand that our jobs, our offices, and the free coffee are only possible as long as we have customers, our purpose is clear. The first two paragraphs of Verizon Wireless's credo are dedicated to establishing the customer as the focal point of all activities in the organization.

## Results

You can spend a lot of time drawing up lists of goals, but if you don't achieve them, you haven't added much value with the process. I always encouraged my teams to plan less and execute more. Extensive planning and deliberating only help your competition. Customers won't wait for you, so getting things done in a timely manner wins out over excessive planning.

> ❝ I always encouraged my teams to plan less and execute more. Extensive planning and deliberating only help your competition. ❞

In fighting for customers, I didn't think of competitors as enemies but rather as challenges for us to do better. During my career, I had multiple opportunities to testify before Congressional subcommittees on telecommunications, and each time I made it a point to praise Congress for opening the telecommunications market to competition because I truly believed that competition made us better. I never doubted my organization's ability to win against all comers, but we wouldn't have delivered superior results or been as great a company without having been challenged every day.

## *People*

When we interviewed job applicants at Verizon Wireless, we looked for past behaviors that were consistent with our credo. In 2008, Verizon Wireless's chief marketing officer, John Stratton, was interviewing an external candidate for a leadership role in marketing. The candidate had a strong résumé, appeared bright, and seemed motivated to take his career to the next level. But something in his approach left John wondering if he could make the transition to Verizon Wireless. At the conclusion of the interview, John escorted the candidate to the lobby, where he asked him to read the Verizon Wireless credo that was hanging on the wall there. John told the candidate that what was written was "literally who we are, what we're all about, and describes exactly the nature of the company you are interviewing to join." John added that "if you are not excited about this, I can guarantee that you will not succeed here." He asked the candidate to think about it overnight and call him in the morning. The next morning, the candidate called, and the two agreed to go their separate ways.

Whenever we brought on someone from the outside, we made sure that person understood what our culture entailed as soon as he or she started work. We spent the first hours of orientation explaining our credo. Senior leaders explained to our recruits how we expected them to behave, and we showed a video of the CEO discussing core values. Explaining our culture first in orientation symbolized that getting ahead in the organization depended on living up to our principles. And as well, before we promoted someone, we made sure that person met our values. Other employees could see that people getting ahead were those who behaved consistently with our principles.

Likewise, when making hiring and promotion decisions, we always considered diversity. In business terms, diversity is essential in any results-focused organization simply because seeing a homogenous workforce makes many customers uncomfortable. People prefer to deal with and buy from companies that employ people like them, so it's good business to hire a diverse workforce. And as pointed out in the Verizon Wireless credo, it's simply the right thing to do.

## *Communication*

In Chapter 8, we discussed the uses and (mostly) misuses of e-mail. We advocate picking up the phone or going directly to someone's office to discuss issues, rather than sending long e-mails and copying others with little direct involvement. Talking one-on-one, rather than convening meetings, is almost always preferable as well. Yet many managers rely on e-mails and conferences instead.

Why?

I think it's because such managers want a paper trail or witnesses to communications with other employees. That way, they're covered in case something goes wrong. Sometimes this need results from a lack of trust in their fellow employees—in some organizations, they may be right to feel this way. The person in the next office could be out to stab them in the back. But let's be clear here: that's not the way I ever wanted to operate, and it shouldn't be the way you want to, either.

So don't.

Your word should be enough. You need to respect and trust everyone in your group, and if you don't, you have to explore replacing the ones you don't. Think of the time spent composing and reading e-mails or listening to blather at meetings. It's a lot more efficient to communicate openly in the first place and rely on others to keep their word, just as you do yours.

I tell people, "When I say I'm going to do something, I'll do it." It takes discipline in demonstrating this principle, and time is necessary for employees to see it in action enough that they replicate your behavior. When you don't have a "blaming" culture, action gets taken and teamwork is established. Without teamwork, people tend to focus only on staying out of trouble. This leads to stalling. When I established a candid and direct communications routine, so did others. The result was the removal of hidden agendas and the ability for teamwork to happen naturally.

I mentioned that I first stated our credo, which I hoped would inspire everyone within the company, at our kickoff meeting in 2004. But rolling it out there was not enough. Our entire senior leadership team and I visited offices around the country and kept repeating the message. We knew it was important for employees everywhere to hear it directly from us. No matter how many times we said it, it was usually the first time listeners were hearing it, and they needed to know we were delivering the same message in each locale.

## *Work Habits*

Bureaucracy is enemy number one of a healthy work culture. I have fought bureaucracy in the business world all my life. Just as bureaucracy reduces simplicity in the work environment, as discussed in Chapter 4, it also fosters an unhealthy work environment.

Bureaucracy works well in the military. In a war setting, you need people to set strategic goals, others to devise tactics to accomplish them, and still others to carry out the plan. Assigning people ranks succeeds here because everyone needs to know who gives the orders. But the modern business organization is not the military. Even if you have many people working for you, you need to think small. That means being able to change course quickly, without going through numerous layers of approval.

I know the perils of bureaucracy; I worked for the old Bell System and saw it firsthand. There were seven levels of supervision in the Bell System (similar to many armies that have seven levels of officers), and you weren't supposed to speak to somebody two levels up unless you had first gone through your immediate supervisor. Not only did this stifle ideas and communication, but it led to infighting about what department should be in charge of what work.

After the government mandated the Bell System breakup in 1983, the new companies fought about who and what went where. The focus was mostly on turf, or which managers would get which empire. The newly organized American Bell failed because it was focused internally, not on what customers wanted.

A robust, results-focused culture can lead to success, but that very success breeds bureaucracy. Managers must be diligent in avoiding bureaucracy and "empire building" as their organization grows. In the fastest-growth days of wireless, when we were seeing the doubling of customers year after year, I paid more attention to how fast we were growing our employees than in years of slower growth.

## OTHER EXAMPLES OF CULTURE IN ACTION

Notice when I said culture is the character of an organization, I didn't limit culture to only large organizations. Culture drives organizations large and small.

Conte's is a restaurant on Witherspoon Street in Princeton, New Jersey, known for two things: thin-crust pizza and good service. On almost any day of the week, people will be lined up waiting for a table, and the long, sports-type bar is almost always crowded—sometimes three or four people deep. Frankly, the venue is not much to behold. Located in what used to be an old family home, its decor is from the 1950s, with Formica-topped, chrome-leg tables and black vinyl–covered chairs arranged mess-hall style on an old tiled floor.

Conte's serves great-tasting pizza (the restaurant promotes it as the "Best Pizza on the Planet"), but its friendly and efficient staff is the difference maker. From the second you walk in the door, you feel welcomed. You are quickly and politely greeted and told how long the wait for a table will be, which is typically not long at all. The staff will even take your order while you are waiting. If you decide to have a drink at the bar while your table is being prepared, you are greeted there and swiftly served as well. Overall, the staff are excellent: in spite of how busy they are, they are always courteous and efficient.

Ciro Baldino is one of Conte's owners and its president. I recently asked him how he would define the culture of his business. He thought for a split second before he responded, "We're all about service. People come here because we have a reputation for great pizza, but they come back because of the service they receive while they're here." Incidentally, Ciro told me he doesn't ask his employees to do anything he can't, or won't, do himself. My wife and I have often observed him cooking pizza, tending bar, waiting on tables, and even washing dishes. His work ethic and passion for service are evident in every one of his employees we've met.

Another example to demonstrate that culture is not limited to large corporations and is critical to small businesses is illustrated by the employees of the Mirror Lake Inn Resort and Spa in the Adirondack Mountains town of Lake Placid, New York. Ed and Lisa Weibrecht, owners of the inn, tell their managers their top three priorities are:

1. To find and hire the right people
2. To train them well and test their training
3. And to manage them by empowering them and holding them accountable for results

(Sounds a lot like many of the same concepts we've discussed in earlier chapters.)

The result is a culture that stresses cleanliness, friendliness, and service. The inn offers 130 rooms and three restaurants, and it has a spa that's almost always busy, but as Ed recently told me, his managers are careful to avoid ever having guests feel they are being rushed. Their clearly stated goal is to provide the best possible service and make guests feel comfortable at all times. To that end, Ed says he tells his restaurant managers that although they may be capable of serving up to 130 dinners per night, he would prefer to limit servings to a much lower number if there is any doubt about their ability to do so with the highest-quality service possible.

On any given day, you will find Ed and Lisa with their sleeves rolled up, working closely with their employees, ensuring that their hotel guests have a comfortable and memorable stay—one that not only brings them back but also has them telling others about their great experience at the inn.

## MISMATCH

People not in harmony with an organization's culture sometimes realize this and leave. Other times, the manager discovers people within the organization who don't share the group's values and has to let those people go. Earlier, I mentioned an Eagle Award winner at Verizon Wireless who falsified contracts and had to be fired, despite his status as an award-winning top performer.

When Frank worked for a consulting company, the top salesman promised a client that he would service the contract personally. The CEO reminded the salesman that he was not qualified as a service consultant. The salesman argued that the client trusted him and wanted him personally to consult, but the president wouldn't yield. When he learned that the salesman had made further promises to the client that he would "find a way" to do service consulting, the president had to fire his best producer because going against the rules and promising more than you could deliver violated the company's culture.

If employees share your values but don't bring results, they can be coached on performance. If they bring results but refuse to share your values, you have a tough decision—in our experience, sooner or later they're going to do something unprincipled and will have to be let go.

In the meantime, they are undermining the culture you are trying to build and maintain, even if that's not their intention.

## DISCOVERING CULTURE

You can often discover an organization's culture quickly. In Chapter 5, I discussed visiting a Verizon facility where there was trash in the parking lot and employees were lounging around outside. By these indicators alone, I could tell what the culture was at this particular facility before I even set foot in the door.

Frank was once hired to facilitate a session on "performance issues" with 20 of a national company's employees. When he arrived at the conference room, one attendee was there waiting for him. "How is the company going to use what we say against us?" was the employee's first question to Frank. This was certainly a sign of distrust. A second employee walked in and said, "My manager told me 10 minutes ago to be here this morning. What's this all about?" Obviously, the manager hadn't displayed accountable behavior because he had done nothing to prepare the employee for the session.

When the rest of the attendees showed up, Frank began the session by simply asking, "What's going on in the company?" The employees jumped all over that question. They cited poor working conditions, including lack of maintenance. They complained their managers did not back them by supporting their ideas and suggestions. One employee also mentioned that he had worked for the company more than 10 years. At the 5- and 10-year employment anniversaries, the company awarded service pins. But instead of holding a ceremony and thanking him for his achievements, the boss just left the pin on his desk.

Frank summarized the problems after an hour and a half and began addressing how to deal with the issues following a break. But the attendees weren't done. They had more problems to talk about. One waved his paycheck in Frank's face and asked, "Could you live on this much money?"

Counting the attendees, Frank reached a total of 27, not the 20 who were supposed to attend. The other 7 were managers, but Frank couldn't tell who they were because they complained as much as the rank and file. They certainly did not cast a positive shadow of the leader.

At lunch, Frank went to the executive who hired him to run the session and said he would have to cancel the rest of the day-and-a-half meeting. He told the executive he couldn't address the performance issues he was hired to deal with until the company fixed basic issues of working conditions and management support. In short, the company's culture did not support a healthy environment, Frank told him, and it would take more than a two-day session to solve problems.

A healthy work culture can also be spotted quickly, sometimes in an unusual way. Frank was hired to conduct a program on "managing conflicts" for managers of a national pharmaceutical company. The company had strong values, one of which was "treating people as you would want to be treated." The company's executives discovered that living by that value was especially difficult in conflict situations, where there were often differing views and ideas about future directions. They felt that the skills of conflict management would be valuable for the managers. This in itself said a lot about the importance the company put on its culture—spending money in order to provide staff with the skills required to live it.

The company had just purchased an old middle school for its training facility. When Frank arrived at the school for his first visit, he found there were numerous entrances that looked like the main entrance. As he approached one of them, a maintenance employee was painting some gutters nearby. Frank was looking around when the employee noticed him and said, "You look like you could use some help!"

Frank asked him whether this was the main entrance where the information booth was located. The employee said it was not. In many cases, an employee in that situation might just point to the front doors and say, "They'll help you inside." Instead, he stopped what he was doing, climbed down from the ladder, and took Frank to the proper entrance a short distance away. He inquired where the session was being held and escorted Frank to the seminar room at the other end of the building. This simple five-minute gesture spoke loudly and clearly about the culture at that pharmaceutical company. The maintenance worker lived by and demonstrated to Frank the value of treating others the way he would like to be treated.

What I intended from the start of my leadership of Verizon Wireless was to build a culture of performance. My role was first and foremost about getting the job done of attracting and keeping customers and winning in the marketplace. In those years, I reread the Verizon credo frequently, to test my own behavior and actions against our stated cultural values. I wanted to make sure I modeled the culture in all my dealings and consistently created a positive shadow as a leader. With our credo clear, people knew they had a job to do; they couldn't let their team down.

## Chapter Summary Points

1. Culture comes from the top.
2. A culture is built around customers, results, people, communication, and work habits.

3. Culture is far more than signs posted, a feel-good climate, or the flavor of the day.

4. If you personally fall short of your culture, take action to correct it as soon as possible.

5. Emphasize your culture in the recruiting and orientation process, and include it in your daily activities.

## Chapter Action Guide

Use all the behaviors, techniques, tools, and skills that we have discussed to formulate your own culture.

# Conclusion

We have written this book to help managers become better leaders, but how do managers actually accomplish this? I don't think they necessarily get better by virtue only of their experience. They also don't get better by just reading a management book like this one or by attending a seminar, although some may think they do. In both these cases, they frequently fail to improve if they don't translate concepts, ideas, and skills into management strengths. The key is the ability to take a concept, idea, or skill and turn it into a daily behavior through commitment and practice: this is the only way you can continue to improve or sustain results.

While I was at Verizon Wireless, "creating a great place to work" was important, but I knew that growing a successful company was the primary goal, and a great workplace was a by-product of achieving it. People understood they could ask questions and get straight answers. They knew bluffing wasn't tolerated; honesty was the key to how we operated with customers, suppliers, and each other. We focused on meeting our goals and shared information on our progress, so everyone knew how we were doing as a company. Accountability for our actions and our individual results was imperative to our success. As a manager, it was also always important not to lose sight of those focal

points that lay the groundwork for any organization: the Four Fundamentals. If our actions did not accomplish these goals, then I knew it
was time to refocus our efforts or change course, and quickly.

You may consider it daunting to build a healthy culture if you are
not the CEO, since change comes from the top. But you can nonetheless instill the right way of doing things in the area you influence—
whether it's a company, department, or division. You can start today by
putting into practice the concepts, skills, and principles in this book.
Begin by reviewing the chapters where we've given you the ingredients
for a results-focused culture. If you follow the guidelines we've suggested, you will get results, and a high-performance culture will follow.

# Endnotes

## CHAPTER 1

1. Joan Koob Cannie, *Take Charge: Success Tactics for Business and Life*, Upper Saddle River, NJ: Prentice Hall Trade, 1980.

## CHAPTER 2

1. Jean Brittain Leslie and Ellen Van Velsor, *A Look at Derailment Today: Europe and North America*, Greensboro, NC: Center for Creative Leadership Press, 1996.
2. Christine Pearson and Christine Porath, *The Cost of Bad Behavior: How Incivility Is Damaging Your Business and What to Do about It*, New York: Portfolio Hardcover, 2009.
3. William Oncken, Jr., *Managing Management Time: Who's Got the Monkey?* Upper Saddle River, NJ: Prentice Hall Trade, 1987.

## CHAPTER 8

1. K. J. McCorry, "Try These Six Steps to Slow Deluge of Unwanted E-mail," *Boulder County Business Report*, August 7, 2009.

# Index

# About the Authors

**Denny Strigl** is the former CEO and president of Verizon Wireless. He is widely recognized as one of the most prominent architects of the wireless communications industry, and his career in telecommunications spans over four decades.

Strigl began his career in 1968 with New York Telephone and held positions at AT&T and Wisconsin Telephone before becoming vice president of American Bell Inc. In 1984 he became president of Ameritech Mobile Communications, where he was instrumental in launching the nation's first cellular telephone network in Chicago. While there, he won the Cellular Industry Achievement Award for engineering advancement and pioneering in marketing programs. He joined Bell Atlantic in 1989, rising to the position of chief operating officer of New Jersey Bell before being named president and CEO of Bell Atlantic Mobile in 1991. He subsequently was named president and CEO of the combined Bell Atlantic Mobile and NYNEX Mobile when those two companies merged in 1995. He went on to become president and CEO of Verizon Wireless and executive vice president of Verizon Communications. On January 1, 2007, Strigl was named president and COO of Verizon Communications, where he remained until his retirement in December 2009. In this capacity, he was responsible for all Verizon's network businesses—Verizon Wireless, Verizon Telecom, Verizon Business, and Verizon Services Operations, which provides financial, real estate, and other functional services to all of the corporation's operations.

Strigl is past chairman (1996–1997) of the board of directors of the Cellular Telecommunications & Internet Association, the national industry association based in Washington, DC. He serves on the board of directors of the Eastman Kodak Company, PNC Financial Services and PNC Bank, and Anadigics, Inc. Strigl holds a degree in business administration from Canisius College, where he recently served as chairman of the board of trustees, and an MBA from Fairleigh Dickinson University, which named him to its Pinnacle Society for Distinguished Alumni. He is an avid skier and aviation enthusiast, and he holds a commercial pilot's license.

❖  ❖  ❖

**Frank Swiatek** is a performance consultant and speaker in the areas of leadership, management, sales, and strategic direction. He has conducted over 3,400 sessions for organizations throughout the United States and Canada over a 30-year period. In addition to running his own firm, he is also an adjunct faculty member at Canisius College in Buffalo, NY. He served as a seminar leader for Learning Dynamics (Boston, MA) and the Waterloo Management Education Centre (Canada) for over 12 years. Frank holds a degree from Canisius College in business administration, where he currently serves on the Board of Regents. He has received the prestigious Certified Speaking Professional (CSP) designation from the National Speakers Association, the highest earned award of the Association. Frank can be reached for speaking engagements at fes52@aol.com.

**DATE DUE**